Balancing Hormones
Naturally

First published in 1994
by ION Press, London.

Editor: AnnA Rushton
Cover design: Jonathan Phillips
Layout: Heather James

ISBN 1 870976 10 X

Printed and bound in Great Britain by
The Bath Press, Avon

balancing hormones
naturally

Kate Neil

**ION
PRESS**

ACKNOWLEDGEMENTS

My thanks go to Dr John Lee, Patrick Holford and Celia Wright for creating the opportunity for this very much needed book to be written. My special thanks go to AnnA Rushton, Heather James and Bharti Makhijani for their untiring support, encouragement and professionalism that brought this book to completion. I also acknowledge the help of Dian Mills, Erica White and above all the support of Martin, my husband and three sons James, Chris and Tim for carrying on without me over this period and supporting wherever they could.

GUIDE TO ABBREVIATED MEASURES

1 gram (g) = 1,000 milligrams (mg) = 1,000,000 micrograms (mcg)
Most vitamins are measured in milligrams or micrograms. Vitamins A, D and E are also measured in International Units (iu), a measurement designed to provide standardisation of the different forms of these vitamins that have different potencies.

1mcg of retinol or 2mcg of beta carotene = 3.3iu of vitamin A
1mcg of vitamin D = 40iu
1mg of vitamin E = approx. 1iu of d-alpha tocopherol
1 pound (lb) = 16 ounces (oz)   2.2lbs = 1 kilogram (kg)
In this book calories means kilocalories (kcals)

2 teaspoons (tsp) = 1 dessertspoon (dsp)
3 teaspoons (tsp) = 1 tablespoon (tbsp)
1.5 dessertspoons = 1 tablespoon (tbsp)
5 ml = 1 teaspoon
10 ml = 1 dessertspoon
15 ml = 1 tablespoon

References

A list of key references from respected scientific literature used in this book is available from the Institute for Optimum Nutrition, 5 Jerdan Place, London, SW6 1BE. Please send 50p and an SAE.

CONTENTS

INTRODUCTION

For the first time since the introduction of the contraceptive pill, and the subsequent massive rise in synthetic hormone use, there are proven natural alternatives available to help prevent and treat most female health problems.

It is only now, forty years later, that the real long-term effects of taking synthetic hormones are being fully realised. Even though some medical researchers back in the 1960's were well aware of the potential side-effects of giving synthetic hormones, those with the power to make final decisions considered that the benefits far outweighed any risks.

Without any doubt the pharmaceutical companies had a lot to gain financially from the widespread prescribing of synthetic hormones. Women of all ages were potential customers. Sex hormones are possible treatments not only for contraception but are used widely as part of infertility programmes, and are regularly recommended in the form of Hormone Replacement Therapy (HRT), to keep the menopause at bay.

With the accepted use of synthetic hormones as reliable contraceptives, research into natural oestrogens and progesterone declined rapidly.

The pharmaceutical companies soon realised that the potential market for synthetic hormones to treat female health problems was abundant. Researching natural oestrogens and progesterone was no longer desirable, as high profits could not be made from the sale of natural unpatentable products.

For sex hormones, natural or synthetic, to be optimally effective it is crucial that they are in balance. Today it is very hard for the body, even under the best of circumstances, to keep the sex hormones balanced. So what is happening to women? We are currently living in a sea of oestrogenic compounds which are found in food, air and water, plastic residues, exhaust fumes and pesticides. We can eat, drink, or breathe them in to the body.

The new problem of oestrogen dominance

Many current female health problems are linked to too much oestrogen in the body. These can include PMS, endometriosis, ovarian cysts, fibroids, breast cancer and menopausal problems Dr John Lee from Sebastopol, California in the USA, has defined a new syndrome 'Oestrogen Dominance' to explain many of these common female conditions. Dr Lee has had nearly two decades of clinical experience in the field of female health, and his published research explains clearly the background to his theory that many women are suffering from the effects of too much oestrogen. He finds that stress, nutritional deficiencies, oestrogenic substances from our environment, and taking synthetic oestrogens combined with a deficiency of progesterone, are the likely contributing factors to the creation of oestrogen dominance.

The role of women

Women play a very powerful and pivotal role in society of which they are largely unaware. The responsibility of nourishing themselves and the family has traditionally always been left to them.

It is only in this last decade that the importance of nutrition is being realised. So much so, that the future health and the survival of the whole human race depends very much upon it.

Largely due to the dominance of men in medicine, and the subordinate role most women have historically played in society, their understanding and acceptance of themselves has been greatly influenced by the ideas of men. I believe that most women have an inherent knowledge of their own natural way of being, and living against that design can create untold stress.

It is time for women to become educated and clear about what is happening to their own bodies, to take responsibility for their health, and live a life that is in harmony with their natural design.

It is my experience in both teaching and advising women about hormones, that their overall understanding is very sketchy. They are usually amazed at the marvellous synchrony that regulates the peaks and troughs of the monthly cycle for around forty years of their life.

Making simple and beneficial changes to your own diet and lifestyle are the first important steps towards balanced hormones and better health.

To help you along the way, there are now available natural hormonal preparations. Taken together with adjustments in diet and lifestyle, these can help restore the natural hormone balance in your body and return you to a state of good, natural health.

How to use this book

Part 1 Understanding Your Body, gives you the basic information you need to maked informed health choices.
Part 2 Hormones in Havoc, explains that synthetic hormones are not the answer for womens health problems.
Part 3 Balancing Hormones Naturally, gives you safe alternative natural strategies for restoring, maintaining and promoting your health.

PART 1

Understanding your body

Women are meant to be in harmony with their bodies. We have developed a natural monthly rhythm where the hormone levels ebb and flow. This is how we were designed and provided our diet, environment and lifestyle conform to our natural design, then no part of the life cycle need be thought of as an illness or a disabling condition.

There are three main hormonal phases in a woman's life: menstruation, pregnancy and menopause. Understanding each phase helps you be in control and make clear decisions about what you most need.

The efficient functioning of the sex hormones progesterone and oestrogens are vital as they play a key role in all stages of the female health cycle. Knowing how they work and what they do is one of the most important pieces of information any woman needs to ensure total hormonal health.

1
THE FEMALE LIFE CYCLE

U ntil relatively recently the bodies of men and women were considered structurally similar. In the 4th century the Bishop of Emesa in Syria wrote 'Women have the same genitalia as men except that theirs are inside the body and not outside it'. In fact it was not until 1890 that medical science began to investigate the workings of the human menstrual cycle.

Since medicine was, and still is, largely dominated by men, the current understanding of the female cycle and female problems is based on the male perspective. The language medical and scientific men used to describe the processes that occur throughout the female life cycle still colour our understanding and attitudes today.

Rarely, if at all, did you find accounts of women's views on what they thought was happening to their bodies. In this way women have come to understand the workings of their body through men. However, by the 1950's women started to question what was happening to them, and as a result the 'natural childbirth' and 'women's rights' movements began to develop.

Attempts to control fertility must be as old as childbirth itself. What is new in the second half of this century is the method of control. For the first time in human history, drugs were used en masse for the purpose of birth control. Although it was known that these drugs would control fertility, the full implications of their effects on health were not fully realised. It is only now that we are beginning to have a good understanding, not only of the effects of these drugs, but of the intricate synchrony of events that control the monthly cycle.

Nature's design

The female pelvis is truly a wonder to behold. It contains the womb, which under the influence of a fine balance of hormones prepares for itself every month a special lining in preparation for a possible pregnancy. If pregnancy does not occur this lining is shed and the process of building up a new lining starts again. The uterus is normally smaller than a fist but can accommodate a baby larger than a football. It contains muscles like no other found in the body, that enable through regular uterine contraction and retraction the successful delivery of a baby and return to normal size within only six weeks. The ovaries are responsible for producing eggs and are enclosed in sacs that are well protected, deep within the pelvic cavity. Nature finds very ingenious ways of ensuring the survival of the species.

The female life cycle - menstruation

The sex hormones in girls remain dormant until the average age of twelve or thirteen. Around then, the hypothalamus, a small gland at the base of the brain, makes a master hormone. This instructs the pituitary gland connected to it to release into the blood two powerful hormones, follicle stimulating hormone (FSH) and luteinizing hormone (LH). These two hormones are responsible for the development and release of an egg from the ovary. When a girl is approaching the onset of her menstrual cycle, the cells of the pituitary gland and ovary are laden with receptors, which become supersensitive for the uptake of these stimulating hormones. It takes about three years for the menstrual cycle to be fully established from the time of the first period. Of the millions of potential mature eggs that are present before birth, only about 300,000 are left at puberty.

The menstrual cycle

It is worth remembering that the only purpose of the monthly menstrual cycle is to ensure the survival of the species. In regular, exquisitely synchronised order, the sex hormones are released into the blood to bring about the release of a mature healthy egg, in the hope that it will meet an equally healthy sperm and become fertilised by it. The cycle repeats itself month after month for around forty years of a woman's life, and is normally only interrupted by pregnancy.

The master controller of this hormone activity is the hypothalamus. It acts like a control centre which shares and integrates many biochemical, immunological and emotional conditions. Menstruation can be affected by emotional states, stress, diet, other hormones, illness and drugs. The average menstrual cyle lasts for 28 days. However, it is not uncommon for cycles to vary between three to six weeks.

From menstruation to ovulation (Days 1 - 14)

At the beginning of a menstrual cycle the levels of the hormones oestrogen and progesterone are very low as a result of the specially prepared womb lining having been shed. The lining was shed because a fully mature egg did not meet a sperm and become fertilised.

The hypothalamus gland senses that the levels of oestrogen and progesterone are low and releases the first master hormone which causes the pituitary gland to release follicle stimulating hormone (FSH). As the name implies the responsibility of FSH is to work on the eggs within the ovary and ripen one ready for release and fertilisation. FSH also causes the ovary to produce oestrogen. The gradual rise of oestrogen over the first half of the cycle brings about the growth of the lining of the womb and breast tissue. This

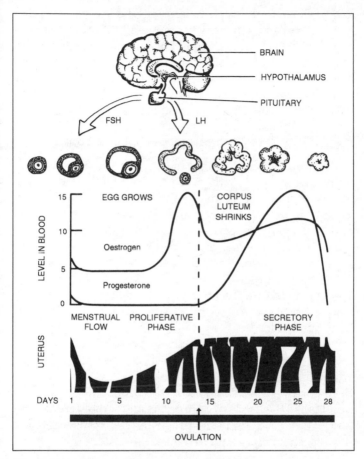

Figure 1: Normal menstrual cycle

process lasts about ten days and is sometimes known as the proliferative stage of the cycle. It is preparing the scene ready for the reception of a fertilised egg.

Follicles are ripening and being prepared in both ovaries. Oestrogen levels peak around day twelve of the cycle which

13

gives a signal to the hypothalamus gland to release another hormone called luteinizing hormone (LH). On day fourteen of a normal cycle a surge of LH occurs which brings about ovulation, the release of a mature egg from the ovary. The egg is now free to enter and move down the fallopian tube attached to the uterus. It is helped by specialised hair- like tissue that assists the egg down the tube to meet the sperm.

From ovulation to menstruation (Days 14 - 28)

The space that is left behind in the ovary after the egg has been released fills with blood and specialised cells and builds up into a dense mass known as the corpus luteum. The corpus luteum now becomes the manufacturing site for both oestrogens and progesterone during the second half of the cycle. High levels of both hormones are required to support fertilisation should it occur.

The rise of progesterone just after ovulation increases body temperature by at least 0.2° centigrade. This is a simple test that many women use to identify whether they have ovulated.

If fertilisation of the egg does not take place the corpus luteum breaks down. The blood vessels supplying the womb lining go into spasm and the lining is shed, forming the menstrual flow. The loss of the corpus luteum causes a rapid fall in the levels of oestrogens and progesterone. This low level of oestrogens and progesterone acts as a signal to the hypothalamus gland to release its master hormone and once again the process starts all over again (see figure 1 on page 13).

The female life cycle: pregnancy

If the egg becomes fertilised, the corpus luteum continues to produce oestrogens and progesterone in large quantities for the next twelve to fourteen weeks, and in small quantities throughout pregnancy. Once the fertilised egg has become embedded in the womb, special cells made by the egg produce another hormone called human chorionic gonadotrophin (hCG).

This hormone stimulates the corpus luteum to continue to grow for the next twelve to fourteen weeks. By this time the placenta is sufficiently developed to take over the production of both oestrogens and progesterone to support the rest of the pregnancy. As the levels of oestrogens and progesterone are so high during pregnancy, the brain does not receive any messages from the egg-stimulating hormone FSH, or the ovulation hormone LH. Oestrogen and progesterone levels do not fall again until the baby is due to be born.

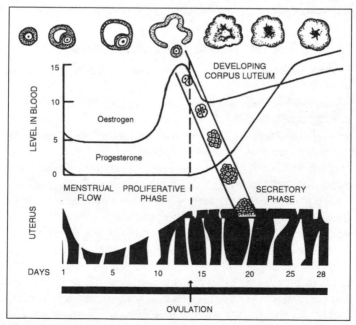

Figure 2: First stage of pregnancy

Hormonal signals, about nine months after the first day of the last period bring about labour (see figure 2 on page 15).

Towards the time of labour, the womb becomes increasingly sensitive to oxytocin, a hormone whose action is stimulated by the pituitary gland. Oxytocin stimulates the uterus to contract, and begins and maintains the process of the delivery of the baby. Labour pains increase under the influence of oxytocin until the baby is born.

After delivery the levels of oestrogen and progesterone rapidly fall. Oestrogen levels remain low, and there is no rise in progesterone in the following months while a new mother is breast feeding. Progesterone is not produced as the mother is not ovulating. Breast feeding is known to be a natural contraceptive, but as the months of feeding increase, it becomes an unreliable form of birth control.

The female life cycle: menopause

The menopause is a process that usually takes about ten years to complete. The menopause, commonly called the 'change of life', refers to the phase which leads up to the last menstrual period and more or less marks the end of reproductive life. This consequently affects the balance of the sex hormones; the ovaries stop producing eggs and making oestrogens and progesterone. This process normally starts around 45 and is usually complete by the age of 55.

At the menopause, women make less oestrogens because they are no longer needed to prepare the womb lining for a pregnancy. As oestrogen levels fall, the menstrual flow becomes lighter and often irregular, until eventually it stops altogether. As the menopause progresses, many cycles occur in which an egg is not released. These are known as anovulatory cycles. Hundreds of eggs vanish each month, and by the time of the menopause only about 1000 are left.

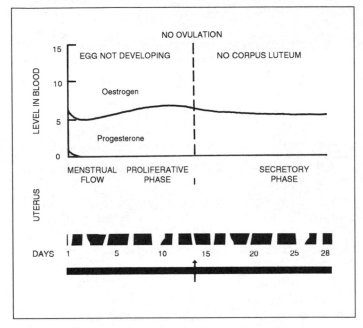

Figure 3: *The menopause*

The change of life should be gradual, allowing the body to adapt to the changes with ease. Because a woman ceases to ovulate, she no longers produces progesterone, so the body compensates by sending a message to the pituitary gland to release increased quantities of FSH and LH. The onset of the menopause is commonly confirmed by an elevation of these two hormones in the blood. (See figure 3 above.)

17

2
PROGESTERONE AND OESTROGENS EXPLAINED

Hormones are messengers. They are made in one part of the body, then released into the blood to affect some distant organ. In order for hormones to respond to the changing needs of the body, it is vital that they can be continually created, broken down and disposed of when no longer needed. This rise and fall of hormones in response to changing needs enables the complex control mechanisms in the brain to work.

The natural design of the body is to produce the two hormones progesterone and oestrogens in balance, so that reproductive ability is maximised. Oestrogens are very similar in their structure to progesterone, and are in fact made from progesterone. These two hormones are closely interrelated in many ways, and although they are generally antagonistic towards each other, each helps the other out by making the cells of a target organ more sensitive.

Understanding progesterone

Progesterone is the hormone that is initially made by the corpus luteum in the ovaries during the latter half of the menstrual cycle. The adrenal glands also produce progesterone in very small amounts. Progesterone is actually made from cholesterol, and cholesterol is produced from the carbohydrates and fats that we eat. Eating the right balance of carbohydrates and fats is the best way to produce the necessary amounts of cholesterol for the production of progesterone by the body and to get this balance right, follow the *Diet for Life* on page 60.

Why we need progesterone

If a woman becomes pregnant, the corpus luteum continues to make progesterone to support the needs of a growing foetus until the placenta is large enough to take over the production of progesterone. It also has many other benefits besides supporting a pregnancy.

In many different ways it helps to keep your weight even. It does this by helping to maintain water balance in the body, thus preventing water retention. It helps the body use fat for energy and is needed for the thyroid hormone to work efficiently. When the thyroid hormone works well it enables the foods that we eat to be burnt effectively, and this also assists weight control.

Progesterone is needed to:

- maintain a healthy sex drive
- build strong bones
- protect against fibrocystic breasts
- protect against breast and endometrial cancer

How progesterone works

For progesterone to do its job as part of the monthly menstrual cycle, it has to get inside the cells of the womb. It travels from the ovary by combining with a protein, which carries it through the blood. As progesterone reaches the cells of the womb it is released from its protein carrier, in order to float through the fatty cell membrane. Once inside the cell, progesterone combines with a receptor and is taken into the nucleus of the cell. The nucleus of the cell contains the final instruction that enables progesterone to do its job of supporting the fertilised ovum and the growing baby. Progesterone makes the womb lining secrete food for the developing egg and suppresses any immune rejection of the baby which contains its father's proteins. If a progesterone receptor is not available to bind with progesterone when it floats into the cell, it will simply float out again. As the menopause approaches, the number of progesterone receptors within the cells decline and a successful pregnancy becomes less viable.

After progesterone has completed its job, it is taken through the blood to the liver and is broken down, inactivated, and disposed of into the digestive tract. The constant production and breaking down of progesterone, in response to the needs of the body from moment to moment, is what controls progesterone balance.

Potential problems

Synthetically prepared progesterone, known as progestogens, are not the real thing. They mimic progesterone, and will fulfill many of its functions, but they are not natural substances that the body recognises. This is the root cause of many of the side effects associated with synthetically prepared progestogens.

Progestogens inhibit the production of natural progesterone. Unlike the synthetic progestogens, natural

Side effects of synthetic progestogens include:	
• regular bleeding	• depression
• nausea	• skin problems
• vomiting	• reduced sex drive
• headaches	• increased risk of coronary
• breast discomfort	heart disease

progesterone is believed by Dr John Lee to have no known serious side-effects.

Sources of progesterone

Apart from that made by the body, there are over 5000 plants which contain natural progesterone-like substances. The Mexican yam is the highest known natural source and it contains diosgenin which is easily converted into progesterone in the body.

Natural progesterone-like preparations derived from the Mexican yam are available to address the imbalance caused by oestrogen dominance.

Understanding oestrogens

Like progesterone, oestrogens are natural, essential hormones that are made by the body when required to perform specific jobs. Unlike progesterone, oestrogen is not one hormone, but a group of hormones that have a similar action. The three most common oestrogens are called oestrone, oestradiol and oestriol. The ovaries are the primary producers of oestrogens. Fat cells and the adrenal glands also produce oestrogens. They become the primary producers of oestrogen during and after the menopause. Keeping the adrenal glands healthy, and not becoming too thin, helps to ease the transition through the menopause.

Why we need oestrogens

During puberty in girls, natural oestrogens encourage the growth and development of the breasts, the uterus, underarm and pubic hair, and the laying down of fat that contributes to the typical female body shape. The lining of the vagina and vaginal secretions are stimulated under the influence of oestrogens which makes sexual intercourse more comfortable. Increased secretions also protect and cleanse the vaginal mucosa.

Once the menstrual cycle has started, oestrogens are responsible in the first two weeks of the cycle for the development of the immature egg into a matured egg. When oestrogen levels peak around day twelve of the cycle it brings about ovulation by stimulating the release of luteinising hormone (LH).

During pregnancy oestriol is produced in significantly larger amounts than either oestrone or oestradiol. However, oestrone and oestradiol predominate during the non-pregnant state. Oestrogens lay down fat cells which ensure that in times of famine pregnant women are able to store fat as a reserve in order to protect their growing baby.

Potential problems

We are all currently experiencing the effects of oestrogen dominance and that can be potentially harmful. Oestrogen dominance can increase water retention, decrease sexual drive, adversely affect blood sugar control and increase the risk of breast and endometrial cancer. Studies have shown that both oestrone and oestradiol increase the risk of breast cancer and that oestriol is protective. Synthetic oestrogens found in contraceptive pills do not contain oestriol, nor are they converted into oestriol in the body. They also inhibit the production of natural hormones.

Oestrogens have been much hailed as preventing osteoporosis, but can at best only retard bone loss. They do not directly help to build bone.

Oestrogen-like compounds are also found in the environment, and these are called xenoestrogens. These usually include petrochemicals, but also include organochlorine compounds like the pesticides DDT and kepone. These chemicals are found everywhere in substances ranging from rainwater to breast milk. Abnormalities in the development of male sexual organs during life in the womb, like undescended testes, are linked to xenoestrogens.

Sources of oestrogens

Many plants contain oestrogen-like compounds that are called phytoestrogens. They are found in soya, particularly tofu and miso, citrus fruits, wheat, licorice, alfalfa, fennel and celery. Soya is the richest source of phytoestrogen. The diet of Japanese women is high in soya. One study showed that such women on a traditional low-fat diet had phyto oestrogen levels in their urine of up to 1000 times higher than American women. Japanese women have a much lower frequency of hot flushes and other menopausal symptoms than Western women.

It is thought that phytoestrogens play a protective role by binding oestrogens made in the body to a protein made in the blood, reducing the amount of oestrogens available to the body. Obesity can decrease the amount of this binding protein in the blood, and increase the amount of available oestrogens.

PART 2

Hormones in havoc

Many of women's current health problems can be traced to the use of powerful synthetic hormones throughout the entire reproductive cycle.

Whatever their purpose, their effect is to totally disrupt the natural balance and interaction of oestrogen and progesterone in the body.

The Pill and HRT both have specific actions on the hormonal system that need to be fully understood so that you can make a clear choice about what you are actually taking, and what the effect, both short and long-term, can be.

Even if you have never taken any form of synthetic hormone, you will still be affected. As a society we are awash in synthetic oestrogens, through the food chain, household and industrial chemicals and plastics, and what may be the most dangerous of all, through our water supply.

Dr John Lee has coined the term oestrogen dominance to describe the current health state of many women, and lies at the root of a growing number of hormonally-linked illnesses.

3
THE PILL AND HRT

With hindsight, it will very likely be recorded in history that the widespread prescribing of synthetic hormones to women was the biggest medical bungle of the century. Many women taking the contraceptive pill and HRT have very little idea about the hormones they are taking, and they certainly don't know how the hormones act. Without a doubt women have been subject to the largest medical experiment of all time.

The Contraceptive Pill (The Pill)

Trying to control fertility has long been a major pre-occupation. What is new since the second world war is not the attempts at fertility control itself, but the much more successful methods available and the form of their control.

Back in the 1960's the time was ripe for effective, guaranteed contraception. Venereal diseases were being effectively treated, and constraining religious beliefs were being eroded. The second world war had changed women's role in society. They replaced men at work and gained important industrial and political skills. Post-war there was no longer the same pressure from society to regulate women's sexuality and the time was right for an effective, available form of contraception.

By the 1960's the social climate was ready for the manufacture and development of the Pill. The market expanded considerably, and greatly to the profit of the pharmaceutical industry. Dr Ellen Grant, author of 'The Bitter Pill' and 'Sexual Chemistry' was an early medical researcher of synthetic hormones and their effects on health. Back in the 1960's she was shocked when synthetic hormones were not withdrawn from the market, due to their known serious side-effects.

How the Pill works

The Pill works by suppressing natural hormones. It interferes with the natural balance of oestrogens and progesterone. The production of luteinising hormone is inhibited, preventing ovulation, and cervical mucus becomes hostile to sperm. The lining of the womb becomes altered, which makes the implantation of an egg difficult.

The Pill stops menstruation, and bleeding only occurs each month because the hormones are not taken for seven days of the cycle. This bleeding would be better termed withdrawal bleeding, not menstruation. The hormonal situation that arises mimics a pregnancy.

Both synthetic oestrogens and progestogens are absorbed very well by the body. They are highly effective due to their ability to act in the body for longer than natural hormones, combined with the fact that they are difficult for the body to break down and get rid of.

How the Pill is made

Contraceptive pills are made in pharmaceutical laboratories, by converting natural progesterone, into a similar but unnatural, substance not recognised by the body. The hormones from which synthetic progestogens are most commonly manufactured originate from natural progesterone-like substances found in foods. Synthetic oestrogens are made chemically in the laboratory.

Contraceptive pill preparations

The Pill contains synthetic progesterone (progestogen) and synthetic oestrogens in variable quantities according to the type of Pill being used. The contraceptive pill is prescribed either as a combined Pill, which contains both synthetic oestrogens and synthetic progestogen, or as a progestogen-only preparation.

The combined pill

This is usually prescribed as a fixed dose over a specific period during the month. Sometimes it is prescribed in a 'phasic' form, whereby the relative amounts of oestrogens and progestogen vary during the month. It is usually easy to know whether you are taking a combined Pill because there is a six or seven day gap when no Pill is taken. However, some preparations are formulated to take a Pill every day, but seven of the Pills are hormoneless. This is considered easier, as the taker does not have to remember when they stopped and when to start taking them again. Combined Pill preparations are usually classified according to the amount of oestrogens they contain, as low or medium dose Pills.

The phasic combined Pills more closely resemble the normal working of the menstrual cycle, but it should be remembered that they are synthetic hormones and, at best, will only simulate a normal menstrual cycle. They will block the action of natural hormones.

Known risks

The combined Pill should not be given to women that presently have, or have previously suffered from, vein or other blood vessel blood clots, liver disease, known or suspected breast cancer, or other hormone dependent cancers and vaginal bleeding of unknown cause. Any history of high blood pressure and obesity makes it inadvisable to take the combined Pill.

Increased risks

Taking the combined Pill increases the risk for coronary artery disease, and this is enhanced in Pill users that smoke.

• You are at increased risk of coronary artery disease if you are obese, have diabetes, a history of several pregnancies, toxaemia of pregnancy and are over 35 years of age.

• Women with a history of epilepsy, migraine, asthma or heart disease may find their symptoms get worse whilst taking the Pill. Changes in brain wave patterns (EEG) are seen in up to 60% of women taking the combined Pill.

Reduced effectiveness

The effectiveness of the combined Pill can be reduced by digestive upsets like diarrhoea and vomiting, the action of some medications, including antibiotics, sedatives, anti-arthritic drugs and anti-epileptic drugs.

A big problem associated with taking the combined Pill is remembering to take it regularly and on time, to ensure maximum contraception. Women have become pregnant whilst taking the Pill. Hormone exposure during early pregnancy has been shown to be potentially harmful to the growing foetus. The combined Pill is not recommended to be taken during pregnancy or whilst breast feeding.

Side-effects include:

• nausea	• depression
• vomiting	• blood clots
• headache	• changes in skin colour
• breast tenderness	• high blood pressure
• weight changes	• loss of periods
• changes in sex drive	

The progestogen-only pill (Minipill)

These only contain a progestogen and a pill is taken every day. Once the regime has started it has to be maintained continually throughout the required time of contraception. It's effectiveness as a contraceptive is high, but lower than that associated with the combined Pill. It is vital to take the progestogen-only Pill regularly at the same time each day to maintain good contraceptive cover. A delay of only three hours can result in a loss of protection. Progestogen-only Pills are sometimes recommended for women who have problems with the combined Pill.

Known risks

The known risks and precautions are similar to those given for the combined Pill.

Side effects include:

- irregular bleeding
- nausea
- vomiting
- headache
- breast discomfort
- depression
- skin problems
- weight gain

A woman should stop the progestogen-only Pill if she experiences a loss of vision or any visual problems, headaches or migraines get worse, or if there is any serious unexplained illness.

Depo-Provera and Noristerat

Depo-Provera and Noristerat are injectable forms of progestogens. They are long-acting and their effects last for eight weeks. They give as good a contraceptive cover as the combined Pill, and are recommended for women who are unable to use other forms of contraception. Ideally they are used for short-term contraceptive cover only, such as after a rubella infection, or before a vasectomy becomes effective. Full counselling should be given prior to being recommended this form of contraception.

Known risks

Provera carries the warning that its use in early pregnancy may increase the risk of early abortion or congenital deformities of the foetus. According to Dr Ellen Grant, when Depo Provera injections were given to mothers for contraception, soon after the birth of their baby, they were often not told what was in their jab or that the hormones would be excreted in their milk and could affect their baby's development.

Be aware - the Pill can kill

It should be understood, that although rare, the Pill can be life-threatening, particularly the combined Pill. It can lead to a fatal blood clot, that ultimately blocks the blood supply in the lungs. Recent studies in Britain indicate that a woman who is on the Pill is twice as likely to experience a fatal blood clot, than non-Pill users. The problem is so worrying that the Family Planning Association launched a public education campaign targeting Britain's three million Pill users. Research shows that many women are still not getting the informationthey need.

Hormone Replacement Therapy (HRT)

Despite research showing the downside of HRT, it has been referred to more than once as the most important preventive medicine of the century. Between 1963 and 1973 sales of oestrogen preparations quadrupled and half the post menopausal female population was using HRT.

British and American doctors were early proponents for recommending HRT to prolong women's active sex lives after the menopause. Ever since it was first introduced, the figures have been manipulated to infer a variety of benefits, including stronger bones and protection from heart disease.

According to the Amarant Trust, a charity that uncritically promotes HRT, the menopause is a 'deficiency disease'. By definition, diseases need to be treated, and that's where HRT comes in.

How HRT works

HRT works by replacing the levels of oestrogens and progesterone that naturally decline in the body, during and after the menopause. The question that really needs to be asked is why women need these hormones to be replaced artificially when nature obviously and clearly intended them to decline at the menopause. Although it is possible for hormone levels to be maintained for longer with an optimum diet in order to continue to have a vital and active sex life.

Known risks

It is thought that low oestrogen levels are responsible for the increased risk for heart disease and osteoporosis in the menopause, and many of the common symptoms that are associated with it including hot flushes, vaginal dryness and depression. Consequently, oestrogen-only HRT preparations were made to solve the problem. The oestrogen-only preparations were soon linked to an increased risk for developing cancer of the womb lining and are now no longer recommended for women who have not had a hysterectomy. Combining oestrogens in HRT with a progestogen appeared to prevent this problem. Now women are recommended a combined HRT preparation, unless they have had a hysterectomy. However, the addition of a progestogen to HRT appears to lower the beneficial effects on blood vessels. Women who experience an early menopause, before the age of 45, either naturally or through surgery, are recommended HRT, as their risk for osteoporosis and heart disease is increased.

Side effects

Generally, the side-effects of HRT are similar to those associated with taking the Pill which are listed on page XX.

Progesterone injections and suppositories have been associated with a few, relatively minor side effects, which include skin problems, weight gain, breast discomfort and PMS symptoms.

Recent surveys indicate that 70% of women stop HRT within a year and only 7% are still taking it after 8 years.

What's available

HRT preparations are available in a variety of forms, pills, patches and implants. They can be taken orally, vaginally, as implants under the skin, and as preparations that are absorbed into the skin. Choosing the most appropriate form of HRT is not straightforward. It is assessed largely according to risk and convenience.

Whilst most HRT preparations use oestrogen-based hormones that are naturally produced by the body, like oestradiol and oestriol, some preparations are based on synthetic oestrogen hormones, like ethynloestradiol. All combined HRT preparations are combined with a synthetic progestogen and not natural progesterone.

Problems associated with HRT preparations

It is not really understood how best to take HRT. Taking oestrogens by mouth is associated with nausea, vomiting, bloating and abdominal cramps. Oral oestrogens go to the liver first for breakdown, so it becomes difficult to know how much will end up in the blood. In fact, the blood levels of women taking identical doses can vary up to 50 times for oestrogens and 10 times for progestogens.

The skin patch bypasses the liver and this this gives a higher level of oestrogens in the blood, but this method is associated with a localised discolouration of the skin.

Oestrogen implants are becoming more popular. This involves a small operation where pellets are inserted under the skin. Implants are associated with an addiction to oestrogens. Implants should last six months but frequently women return 3-9 weeks later comoplaining of recurring menopausal symptoms. It has been suggested that women who gain such a tolerance to oestrogen patches have psychiatric problems, and require larger than normal amounts of oestrogen!

Professor Howard Jacobs of the Middlesex Hospital in London suggests that it may be that the oestrogen sensitive cells in the bodies of women continually blasted with high doses of the hormone have lost the ability to respond accordingly. It is also indicated that early use of oestrogens whether from the contraceptive pill, HRT or in the control of PMS, may set the stage for an increased need for replacement therapy. Dr Ellen Grant describes this constant level of oestrogen as being like a car that is stuck in a single gear. It is possible that HRT creates articially high levels of oestrogen in the body and this can trigger a hormone 'crash' if those levels fall even a small amount and this could make ordinary menopausal symptoms get worse.

Another problem with oestrogen implants is that for two years after stopping the drug, there is still a risk of developing endometrial cancer. It is now generally acknowledged that using oestrogen-only HRT can increase the chances of a woman developing endometrial cancer twenty times, after several years. To lower the risk, a woman needs to take a progestogen for two years or more after discontinuing an oestrogen implant.

Natural help

The time of the menopause provides an excellent opportunity for doctors to educate their patients about diet and lifestyle. HRT should not be the first treatment of choice. The use of the Pill for women's health problems is essentially inappropriate, although its effectiveness as a contraceptive cannot be denied. Addressing the diet and lifestyle is the first place to start. Where hormone therapy is indicated it should be with natural hormones.

Dr John Lee has long-term experience in treating women with natural progesterone for many of their health problems, including PMS, endometriosis, fibroids as well as those linked with the menopause. He has said that women should be upset that the balancing of their hormones uses synthetic and abnormal versions of the real goods, particularly when natural hormones are available, safer and more appropriate for their bodies.

4
SYNTHETIC HORMONES: EXPLODING THE MYTHS

In real terms, I believe, it is virtually impossible for synthetic hormones to restore natural hormonal balance in the body. At best they can only simulate what natural hormones should be doing. One of the main problems over the past thirty years has been the steadily-promoted belief that synthetic hormones are the answer to all womens health problems, but is it really the case?

Myth Number 1: The Pill as problem-free contraception. It certainly has given women effective contraception, but the problems can include a body depleted of vital nutrients, difficulty re-establishing a normal menstrual cycle, problems in conceiving, raised blood pressure, risk of fatal blood clot, and a higher risk for certain types of cancer.

Myth Number 2: HRT as a complete 'cure' for the menopause. Given to relieve symptoms such as hot flushes, vaginal dryness and loss of libido, HRT causes as many problems as it relieves Menopause is a natural stage of life, not an illness, and many of it's effects are easily treated through attention to lifestyle and diet. HRT is claimed to increase bone density to avoid the perils of osteoporosis, protect against the risk of coronary heart disease and lower blood pressure, but this has not been convincingly proved.

What is known is that HRT carries an increased risk for both breast and endomentrial cancer and has not been in use long enough to be properly evaluated for it's long-term effects on health.

Typical Problems of Hormone Imbalance:

- PMS
- weight gain
- breast lumps
- breast cancer
- ovarian cysts
- osteoporosis

- hot flushes
- vaginal dryness
- menopausal problems
- fibroids
- endometrial cancer

Sex hormones, whether natural or synthetic, are potent substances that have widespread effects. The important thing is keeping them in balance. If progesterone and oestrogens are kept within optimal balance they should promote health, not create health problems.

Upsetting the fine balance of natural hormones can result in devastating symptoms and health problems. Deficiencies and excesses in diet, physical and emotional stress, and exposure to hormones through the food chain, environment or synthetic medications, can all influence the balance. For most women, the imbalance usually results in there being too much oestrogen in relation to progesterone.

Currently, the popular way to deal with problems associated with natural hormonal imbalances is through the use of synthetic hormones. Very often it has been through using synthetic hormones, usually for contraception or infertility, that imbalances have occurred in the first place. It is very unusual for a woman to be advised about her diet and lifestyle as a means of correcting hormonal imbalances although this is the most obvious and effective place to start the process of rebalancing the body naturally.

Addressing the issue

The widespread use of the contraceptive pill and HRT for the treatment of health problems, does not address the real issues behind the development of heart disease and osteoporosis in Britain. At best it is a short-term unnatural answer to a long-term problem.

Heart disease, osteoporosis and many of the symptoms experienced during the menopause are linked to a variety of other factors including diet and lifestyle, not just too little oestrogen. Research shows that women from cultures eating a natural diet and maintaining a healthy lifestyle have little evidence of heart disease and osteoporosis past the menopause. It is likely that many of the causes that bring about an early menopause could be prevented by a change in diet and lifestyle as early in life as possible.

Hormone replacement therapy during the menopause will soon be one of the major areas of preventive medicine in our society. However, the effects of synthetic oestrogens in combination with different progestogens on coronary heart disease, blood pressure, blood clotting, and bone density have not been investigated adequately.

The fundamental problem

Synthetic hormones are very similar in their structure to natural hormones. The body will accept them and they will perform many of the important functions of natural hormones. They will bind with the same receptor sites in target cells, but may convey an altered message to the natural hormones. Synthetic hormones are not so easily adjusted or as easily disposed of by the body. They are **not** equivalent to natural hormones. Women given identical amounts of synthetic hormones were found when tested to have variable levels in their blood of up to fifty times more for oestrogens and ten times more for progestogens.

Fertility

Many women have spent years on the Pill, a method of contraception that works by preventing ovulation. For one in every two hundred women their periods will cease after stopping the Pill. Fertility will return in most cases before two years.

As part of an infertility programme, many women are treated with drugs to stimulate ovulation, even when they can be shown to be ovulating spontaneously. Often these are the same women that had previously taken the Pill. What is often not considered as part of most infertility treatments is that natural hormone production and hormone receptor sites within the cells need a good supply of zinc and magnesium to work effectively. The Pill often depletes the body of these two vital minerals. This problem of low levels of zinc and magnesium is compounded by the perpetual stimulating of multiple eggs to develop cycle after cycle to initiate ovulation. Zinc is vital at every level of fertility.

Pregnancy

The use of synthetic hormones before and during pregnancy and through lactation exposes a developing baby at its most critical stages of development. It is a time when sex, intelligence and future health are being determined. It is known that hormones taken by the mother in early pregnancy can cause cancer and genital abnormalities in her children. The results of a study involving 5,700 pregnancies showed a remarkably low incidence of congenital abnormalities in children born to women that had never taken the Pill, compared to women who had regularly taken it. The risk of limb defects increased 23 times in babies born to mothers who took hormones in pregnancy. Research with animals suggests that exposure to hormones in the womb can cause future breast and ovarian cancers, and giving hormones after the animal has reached maturity can compound these effects. Women exposed to extra hormones in their mother's womb through her use of the Pill and fertility stimulants, may themselves stop ovulating in their twenties and thirties.

There are other more natural ways to control fertility. I am sure that most people, if they fully understood the implications not only to their health, but the health of their child, and ultimately the future health of humanity would choose to take this risk.

Menstrual problems

The Pill is undoubtedly a successful means of contraception. It is also commonly recommended as a treatment for PMS, severe period pains, heavy bleeding, endometriosis and irregular periods.

There is no physiological basis for using the Pill to treat PMS. The Pill does not address the underlying problems associated with heavy bleeding and irregular periods. It stops menstruation, and bleeding only occurs each month because the hormones are not taken for seven days of the cycle. This bleeding would be better termed withdrawal bleeding, not menstruation.

There is sufficient evidence to date to indicate that approaching these problems by improving diet and lifestyle offers a safe and effective alternative to synthetic hormones.

Depression

Women have been classified as hysterical throughout our history. In fact, the term 'hysteria' is derived from the Greek work 'hystera' meaning uterus (womb). Hysteria in the 19th century was considered a condition unique to women.

Our mood is very much dependent on the foods that we eat. The breakdown of protein foods are needed to make neurotransmitters, the brain chemicals whose balance very much controls our mood. Protein breaks down to form amino acids and amines. Cheese, red wine and chocolate contain high levels of amines which can exert a powerful, stimulating, and often immediate action on the brain. If high levels of amines are not broken down, or if the amines are stimulated, they can lead to depression. Enzymes that break amines down require zinc, magnesium and B vitamins. One specialised type of enzyme known as MAO, plays a large role in the breakdown of amines.

Oestrogens and MAO enzymes

Progestogens can stimulate MAO enzymes, preventing them from being broken down, which can cause depression. However, oestrogens generally suppress MAO enzymes and enhance the feeling of well-being. Care needs to be taken with oestrogen though, as too much oestrogen can make the MAO enzymes too sluggish. This in turn can give rise to problems like headaches, migraines, high blood pressure and feeling manic. Women taking oestrogens, as well as psychiatric drugs for depression, such as the tricyclic anti-depressants, which can also change amine levels, should take extra care. Their combined action can prove very powerful. Dr Ellen Grant has said that 'When higher than expected rates of attempted suicide and violent deaths were recorded among HRT takers, the excuse was that more women suffering from depression are put on oestrogens in an attempt to treat them.' Oestrogens are rarely considered as an implicating factor in depressive behaviour.

This example highlights the possible problems that can occur when oestrogens and progesterone are out of balance. How progestogens can interfere with the subtle balance of our brain chemicals and the potential effects of too much oestrogens. Just as importantly, it shows how what we eat can affect our mental well-being. Taking all these factors into account, there is plenty of room for manoeuvre to enhance our well-being naturally without resorting to the synthetic hormones.

CANCER

Cervical Cancer: The cells of the cervix are extremely hormone-sensitive. Levels of progestogen low enough not to alter the cells of the lining of the womb,have been shown to change the cells lining the cervix. Progestogens dry up cervical secretions, and this may be part of the reason why cancer of the cervix develops quickly in the presence of cervical infections.

Skin Cancer: It was predicted in the 1960's that the Pill would increase the chances of a woman developing a melanoma, the most lethal of all skin cancers. Hormones control the pigmentation of our skin and melanoma cancer cells have oestrogen receptors which can make the growth of a cancer more likely. Women taking HRT are also more likely to develop melanomas than the average woman.

Endometrial Cancer: The realisation that oestrogen-only HRT could increase the risk a woman developing endometrial cancer, was the first life-threatening health problem acknowledged with taking HRT. It is now also known that if a woman who has not had a hysterectomy is given only oestrogen it can increase her chance of developing endometrial cancer up to twenty times. The risk increases with the length of time a woman has taken HRT. Oestrogens cause a rapid growth of endometrial cells, which could encourage cancer growth. To limit this potential of

41

developing endometrial cancer when taking oestrogen-only HRT, a progestogen was recommended to be taken with it. When post-menopausal women were tested with combined hormone therapy, it was found that endometrial cancer could largely be prevented. However, one of the side effects of taking progestogen is withdrawal bleeding. This is treated by giving continuous progestogen. Continuous progestogen can lead to breakthrough bleeding, which ultimately can negate the protective effects against endometrial cancer.

The conclusion was that women who have not had a hysterectomy should always receive oestrogens alongside progesterone or a progestogen to prevent endometrial cancer. The effect of this was to increase the market for progestogens to include all women, whether menstruating or post-menopausal.

Breast Cancer: The New England Medical Journal reported that 'studies over a six-year period have shown that the longer HRT is taken there is a fourfold increased risk for developing breast cancer.' Progestogens also assist the development of blood vessels which may encourage the spread of cancer. However, natural progesterone protects against breast cancer.

Tamoxifen

The anti-oestrogen drug Tamoxifen is commonly prescribed to women with breast cancer, and for many healthy women with a high risk for developing breast cancer. Tamoxifen is carcinogenic and can cause an early menopause, osteoporosis, endometrial and liver cancer and clotting diseases. Taking 20mg of Tamoxifen a day can increase the risk for developing endometrial cancer by up to five times. Clotting disorders are seven times more frequent. One study showed just a meagre 0.7% benefit for women taking Tamoxifen preventively, to reduce the risk of developing further tumours in the breasts. Some researchers conclude that Tamoxifen fails to meet the safety standards required for a primary prevention measure. However, it is less toxic than conventional chemotherapy used to treat cancer.

Blood pressure

The effect of synthetic oestrogens and progestogens on blood pressure is not currently fully realised. Oestrogens and progestogens can cause the body to retain salt and water in the cells. This can ultimately raise blood pressure. Research has shown that when four different progestogens were assessed for their ability to rid salt from the body, each of them were actually found to cause salt retention. When progestogens are combined with oestrogens there is an increased risk for developing high blood pressure. Natural progesterone helps to rid the body of excess sodium (salt). This is an example of the difference between natural progesterone and a synthetic progestogen.

Synthetic hormones potentially block the natural ability of the body to use beneficial substances that help keep the blood thin. Women taking oral contraceptives or HRT are more likely to have 'sticky' blood and develop blood clots. Thick blood is also a risk factor for high blood pressure. High blood pressure is a risk factor for developing cardiovascular disease.

Cardiovascular disease

One of the most hailed benefits for taking HRT is that it will considerably reduce the risk of developing heart disease after the menopause. Oestrogen levels seriously decline after the menopause, and oestrogens are considered to be protective to blood vessels and blood fat levels. It is claimed that women taking HRT had half the risk for developing heart disease, and were less likely to die from that cause than the population as a whole.

But this claim does not stand up to close examination. Research indicates that women who take oestrogens after the menopause are more likely to be upper middle class, educated, non-smokers and better fed, all factors that automatically carry a lower risk for developing heart disease, unlike many of the women that do not opt for HRT. A UK review in 1991 concluded that the evidence that HRT is protective against heart disease is weak or non-existent. Making optimistic claims for its benefits are often meaningless because so few women remain long-term users of HRT. Surveys report that 70% of women discontinue HRT within a year and only 7% last eight years.

Increasing the risk

Some studies, in fact, suggest that using HRT actually increases the risk for developing heart disease. All these trials were conducted on women taking the oestrogen-only HRT preparation. Oestrogens are understood to be beneficial for the blood vessels. However, it remains unclear whether the ability of oestrogens to relax arteries is particularly significant in treating heart disease. As the absorption of oestrogens are also variable in different women it has been shown that when absorption of oestrogens are low the diameter of arteries remained unchanged.

Progestogens were added to HRT preparations to minimise the risk of developing cancer of the lining of the womb. However, progestogens reduce some of the beneficial effects of oestrogens on blood fat levels. The protection from heart disease is potentially lost when a progestogen is added to the HRT. However, natural progesterone is beneficial to the cardiovascular system. A study in 1989 found that when women were given a combination of oestrogens and progesterone their blood fat profile improved.

Osteoporosis

The New England Journal of Medicine reported in October 1993 the latest results of an ongoing study of women in Framingham, Massachusetts, USA They said that 'It shows that HRT fails to protect women from osteoporosis - therefore eliminating at a stroke one of the main reasons for its use.'

One study researching 670 women, of whom nearly a third were taking oestrogen therapy, found that bone mass was only preserved in those women that had taken the therapy for seven years or more. Only women that had taken oestrogens for seven to ten years or more had significantly higher bone mineral density than women who had taken oestrogens for a lesser period of time. As only 7% of women are still taking HRT after eight years, this offers little protection against osteoporosis for most women that take HRT.

More startling is the fact that even those women who have taken HRT for ten years are still not protected from fractures due to the thinning of the bones associated with osteoporosis. When these women stopped taking HRT, there was a rapid decline in bone mineral density. By the age of 75, bone mineral density was found to be only 3.2% higher than in those women that had never taken HRT. The osteoporotic process takes time. Most women are not at risk of developing fractures until they are around 80 years old. Therefore, unless you take HRT for life, it will not protect you against the ravages of osteoporosis. However, the longer you take HRT the greater the risk you have for developing breast and endometrial cancer.

Thick, 'sticky' blood may also complicate bone formation. Dr Kitty Little, from Oxford found masses of tiny clots in the bones of rabbits treated with hormones. She is convinced that HRT in the form of oestrogens and progestogen will increase the risk for osteoporosis. Blood clots originate from sticky clumps of platelet cells in the blood. She believes that blood clots in the bones can cause bone to break down, leading to osteoporosis.

When you understand a little about how bones work it is not surprising that HRT fails to give significant protection against osteoporosis. Oestrogens should not be expected to increase bone mass. At best oestrogens will only prevent any further loss of bone. Bone forming cells are of two different types. One type are called osteoclasts, and their job is to travel through the bone in search of old bone that is in need of renewal. Osteoclasts dissolve bone and leave behind tiny unfilled spaces. Osteoblasts move into these spaces in order to build new bone. A lack of oestrogens, as experienced at the menopause, indirectly stimulates the growth of osteoclasts, increasing the risk for developing osteoporosis. HRT containing oestrogen should therefore help prevent osteoporosis. From this point of view it does. However, osteoclast cells have not been shown to have any oestrogen receptors in themselves, so cannot directly build new bone. On the other hand osteoblast cells, which make new bone, have been shown to have not oestrogen, but progesterone receptors. Progesterone, not oestrogen, is the hormone which helps build bone.

5

THE OESTROGEN CONTROVERSY

The potentially devastating effect of synthetic oestrogens is far too serious to be ignored. Its implications could affect each of us, our children, grandchildren, and indeed the future health of generations to come. With knowledge, we can take the right action to help ensure a healthier, brighter future for ourselves and others.

Oestrogen dominance

As we have seen, oestrogens are necessary and vital hormones for the proper functioning of so many activities in the body. Our body needs oestrogen, but it needs it in its natural form so that it can function properly without interfering with any other hormone activity, particularly that of progesterone. The explosion of synthetic hormones into so many areas of our lives is what has brought us to the state that Dr John Lee has described as oestrogen dominance.

We are currently living in a sea of oestrogens. We make them, eat them, take them in the form of medications, drink them and breathe them into the body. There is also widespread exposure to oestrogens from taking natural and synthetic sex hormones for contraception, HRT, infertility, endometriosis and other female health problems.

This continual over-exposure to oestrogens disrupts the balance of our natural body oestrogens, which ultimately affects the working of other hormones, particularly the sex hormone progesterone.

Oestrogen dominance in women

It is vital that women understand the implications of this potentially major health problem, not only for themselves, but for the future health of their children. The incidence of some abnormalities of the reproductive system in baby boys has trebled in the last 30 to 40 years. Research has implicated the exposure to oestrogens in the womb as being the prime suspect for this increase.

Health problems associated with too much oestrogen include:

• PMS	• fibroids
• depression	• breast cancer
• loss of sex drive	• endometrial cancer
• sweet cravings	• vaginitis
• heavy or irregular periods	• weight gain
• fibrocystic breasts	• water retention
• breast swelling	• osteoporosis

When oestrogen levels are normal and in balance with progesterone, it should not create a health problem, in fact balanced hormones should promote health.

According to Dr John Lee, many of these common health problems can be offset by increasing the level of natural progesterone. The problem is not always that progesterone levels are actually lower than normal, but are low in comparison to oestrogens.

In addition to unavoidable exposure to oestrogenic substances found in the environment, women become more exposed to oestrogens made in the body from their mid-thirties onwards. Around this time women do not ovulate with every menstrual cycle. The frequency of such cycles, known as anovulatory cycles (see figure 4), increases as the menopause approaches. The result of this is that progesterone is not produced in response to ovulation. Stress, nutritional problems and chemical pollutants are all possible reasons for anovulatory cycles. It is often possible to detect an anovulatory period due to a change in pattern. The menstrual loss may be heavier or longer.

Due to the regular occurrence of anovulatory cycles before the menopause, oestrogen levels become increasingly dominant. This can lead to the exaggerated symptoms of too much oestrogen experienced before the menopause. This is compounded by the fact that the pituitary gland is

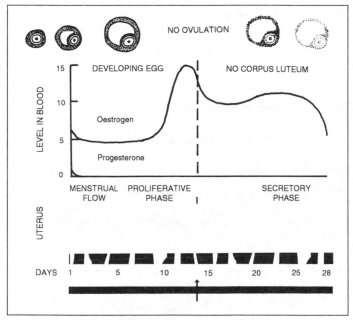

Figure 4: Failure to ovulate due to oestrogen dominance

instructed to release high levels of FSH and LH in response to a low level of progesterone. This can lead to an increased production of oestrogens. Balancing oestrogens with natural progesterone helps to correct the normal control mechanisms in the brain.

Problems associated with oestrogen dominance

Either short or long menstrual cycles can result in oestrogen dominance. The first half of the cycle can last anything from the normal fourteen days and, not uncommonly, up to six weeks. The second half of the cycle is more constant, and usually lasts between ten and sixteen days. The average cycle for instance matures the egg in around fourteen days, but a six week cycle would indicate that it had taken four weeks to mature an egg under the influence of oestrogens. Oestrogen dominance is more likely to arise in the second half of the cycle due to the fact that progesterone is around for a shorter period of time in relation to oestrogen.

Breast cancer is strongly associated with too much oestrogen. The most common time for breast cancer to develop is five years before the menopause when oestrogen dominance is potentially at its highest, due to anovulatory cycles.

Endometrial cancer of the lining of the womb has only one known cause and that is unopposed oestrogens.

PMS is strongly associated with hormonal imbalance. It is a syndrome that presents with a multitude of symptoms that often appear diverse and unrelated. The symptoms of PMS are very similar to those associated with too much oestrogen. Dr Lee found that women who used natural progesterone during the second half of their cycle showed considerable improvements in their symptoms.

An underactive thyroid gland can give rise to a similar set of symptoms as those of oestrogen dominance and PMS. It is known that too much oestrogen affects the thyroid hormone which is responsible for regulating the rate at which foods are utilised by the body.

Blood sugar levels are affected by the presence of too much oestrogens. The symptoms of blood sugar imbalance are in many ways synonymous with oestrogen dominance, PMS and thyroid problems. The hormones insulin, glucagon and the stress hormone adrenalin all control blood sugar levels. Stress hormones are made from progesterone in the body. A low level of progesterone can affect adversely affect how we cope with stress.

All hormones are very much dependent upon each other to maintain the balance of the whole body. If an imbalance arises in one hormone, it is likely to ultimately affect the balance of other hormones.

Oestrogen excess in men

Men naturally produce small quantities of oestrogens. However, they are also exposed to the same level of environmental oestrogens as women. As male body tissues are unused to the presence of oestrogens, the effects of having too much are likely to be very profound. This indeed appears to be the case as increasing evidence shows just what has happened to male reproductive health and fertility in the last fifty years.

Sperm production has dropped a massive 50%.

Sperm quality and the volume of semen have declined.

Undescended testes that fail to descend into the scrotum is a condition that is now three times more common than it was 30 to 40 years ago.

Serious developmental abnormalities of the male sexual organs are increasing.

Cancer of the testes has trebled in Britain.

These effects are potentially devastating for future population health and growth. Without a good supply of healthy, active sperm a man's ability to reproduce is seriously compromised and some scientists believe that if the decline in sperm production continues at the same rate then we could be in danger of becoming extinct .

Oestrogens in the environment

As a result of very rigorous research it has been found that potent oestrogenic substances in the environment are potentially capable of causing many of the problems associated with oestrogen excess, particularly in men.

This important clue resulted by chance. American researchers studying breast cancer cells found that the cells were growing prolifically as though they were exposed to some form of oestrogen. After a thorough process of investigation and elimination they found an oestrogenic substance was leaching from the plastic tubes used to store blood serum, and they identified the chemical as nonylphenol.

This chemical is widely used to protect plastics from oxidation in the plastics industry. Nonylphenol is a versatile substance that binds easily with fats, making it ideal for use in paints, detergents, lubricating oils, toiletries, spermicide foams, agrochemicals and many other products.

Nonylphenol is difficult to get rid of and persists in the environment or a long time. It is stored easily in the fatty tissues of animals. Up to one third is estimated to end up in rivers and lakes. Nonylphenols have been in widespread use for around 40 years.

Nonylphenols and fertility

Fish in Britain and America are found to be showing serious reproductive problems similar to those found in man. The National Rivers Association found that nonylphenols were present in some rivers at levels shown to be very oestrogenic to fish. This poses the question whether nonylphenols could be getting through to drinking water and be responsible for the reproductive changes seen in men over the past 50 years.

The Paris Commission, the international body which sets standards for water quality in France, has already recommended that nonylphenols be phased out by the year 2000, because of their toxicity to aquatic life and their persistence in the environment.

Whilst nonylphenols are the prime suspect due to their proven potency, other sources of oestrogens that developing male babies, growing boys and men are currently exposed to are considered to be contributing to the problem.

Reproductive abnormalities

It is known that potent oestrogenic substances can increase the risk of reproductive abnormalities in humans. Between the 1950's through to the 1980's up to 6 million babies were exposed to synthetic oestrogen, in the form of Di-ethyl-stilboestrol (DES), which was given to pregnant mothers to prevent miscarriage. DES is a very potent synthetic hormone. Studies on male babies born during that period showed a predicted increase in abnormalities of their reproductive organs. The reproductive systems of female babies born over this period, have also been shown to have been adversely affected by DES too.

The list of oestrogenic substances in the environment is growing all the time and are found in common use throughout industry and in the home. They include:

Pesticides - DDT DDE Kelthane Heptachlor Kepan
Industrial chemicals - PCB's and Bisphenol A, Nonylphenols

The whole problem of over-exposure to all forms of oestrogens is likely to remain controversial for some time. Synthetic oestrogens have become a fact of life for so many people, often in ways that they may have been unaware of. We are under continued attack from a whole range of sources of synthetic oestrogens whether chemical or pollutant. Whether finally proven to be the cause or not for many of the serious health problems outlined here, it is wise to limit your exposure to them as much as possible.

PART 3

Balancing hormones naturally

R arely today do you hear women speak of how well they feel. Too many women expect to put up with feeling tired, suffering from PMT and resorting to HRT or even tranquillisers. Feeling just 'all right' isn't good enough. Good health is not an aberration, it is every woman's right.

Today, perhaps more than ever before, women are under a great deal of pressure. They have the responsibility of taking care of their families, their homes, and often have full or part-time jobs as well. All of this takes a toll on general health, and contributes to the problem of hormonal imbalances, together with environmental and dietary factors.

Your health and ability to balance hormones depends on good nutrition. It is not a case of a 'quick fix'. What is needed is a completely different approach to taking care of yourself on a daily basis. Such a diet and lifestyle is the only sure way to a lifetime of health and vitality.

6
NATURAL HORMONES - THE SAFE ALTERNATIVE

Natural hormones are essential substances that have widespread effects in the body. When in normal balance they help to keep us fit and healthy. They know exactly what to do, and when and where. The cells of the body recognise natural hormones and respond to them appropriately.

Progesterone is a key hormone from which oestrogens are made. Almost everything in the body ultimately is made from the food that we eat. Therefore, to make nature's hormones work best for us, it is sensible to provide our body with the best raw materials possible.

The benefits of natural hormones

• The body recognises them and knows exactly how to use them and dispose of them.

• They have been used therapeutically for two decades with good results for many female health problems.

• Natural progesterone preparations have been shown to help redress the problem of oestrogen dominance.

• Women living on the Trobriand Islands near New Guinea are renowned for their health and for enjoying life. They are mostly thin, happy, enjoy wonderful health and a vigorous sex life and do not have large families. Their diet is high in the richest known source of progesterone, the wild yam. Progesterone is the basis for oral contraceptives, which helps to explain why they bear few children.

Natural sources of oestrogens and progesterone

The ovaries are the main source of both oestrogens and progesterone during reproductive life. The corpus luteum of sows was the original medical source of progesterone.

The placenta is a rich source of oestrogens and progesterone during pregnancy. It was common practice to freeze placentas and send them to pharmaceutical companies to extract natural progesterone for medical use.

The adrenal glands and fat cells are the main sources of oestrogens during and after the menopause. Progesterone levels fall to virtually zero at this time.

Many plants contain natural oestrogen and progesterone-like substances. Pharmaceutical companies convert these natural progesterone-like substances into natural progesterone and then into synthetic progesterone.

Plants rich in oestrogen-like substances include soya beans, anise, celery, ginseng, alfalfa, red clover, licorice, rhubarb.

The richest source of progesterone-like substances is the wild yam. Herbs like dong quai, black cohosh and fennel contain active progesterone and oestrogen-like substances.

Natural oestrogen and progesterone preparations are available in the form of tablets, oils and creams.

The uses of natural hormone preparations

On the basis of what we know so far about synthetic oestrogens, it may seem as if oestrogens themselves have little to offer us. However, there appears to be good news about oestrogen-like substances, called phytoestrogens, found in plants. Phytoestogens are thought to stimulate the production of a protein that binds with oestrogens in the blood, resulting in less oestrogen being available to the body.

Creams and tablets containing natural oestrogen-like substances have been used to successfully treat menopausal symptoms such as vaginal dryness and hot flushes. The tableted form has been shown to minimise oestrogen withdrawal symptoms for women who have had problems on HRT. According to naturopath Harold Gaier, the tablet form has no known side effects. Some doctors estimate that between 10 - 15% of their patients do need extra oestrogen as well as natural progesterone to help alleviate persistent menopausal symptoms.

Creams and oils containing natural progesterone-like substances have been shown to help overcome a variety of female health problems including infertility, PMS, weight gain, ovarian cysts, endometriosis, fibroids, fibrocystic breasts, vaginal dryness, hot flushes and osteoporosis. In addition, natural progesterone can reduce the need for oestrogen preparations as it sensitises cells that take up oestrogens. According to Dr John Lee, natural progesterone has no known side effects.

When hormone therapy is required, natural hormones should be the choice, combined with an optimum diet and any necessary lifestyle changes.

7
THE DIET FOR LIFE

The diet for life is one that provides every single cell in the body with the best supply of nutrients. This is the foundation of health. When the diets of other cultures renowned for living to ripe old ages are examined, it is clear that these people eat a varied and natural diet.

The *Diet For Life* aims to give you maximum hormone health; when your hormones are balanced and healthy then the rest of your body should be healthy too.

The basis of the *Diet For Life* is plenty of complex carbohydrates, moderate amounts of protein, a minimum of fats and lots of water. The *Diet For Life* will also give you good levels of vitamins and minerals.

Carbohydrates

Carbohydrates are of two types: complex and simple. They are used by the body to produce energy.

Complex carbohydrates form the basis of the *Diet For Life*. The benefit of eating complex carbohydrates is that it takes time for the digestive tract to break them down to simple substances that the body can use to make energy. Fruit is somewhere between a complex and a simple carbohydrate. The fibre with which fruit is bound is a complex carbohydrate, but the carbohydrates within the fruit itself, (fruit sugar), are relatively simple and easily digested.

The benefit of the fibre is that it helps to control how quickly the sugar from the fruit is released into the blood. Eating a whole piece of fruit benefits the body more than drinking fruit juice because you are getting the fibre as well.

The Diet For Life

Food Group	Best Sources
Carbohydrates	Beans,lentils, wholegrains, vegetables, fruit
Protein	Nuts, seeds, beans, lentils, wholegrains, vegetables, fish, low-fat dairy foods, free range eggs, free range chicken
Fats	Nuts, seeds, cold pressed vegetable oils, oily fish, wholegrains
Water	filtered water, still bottled water, fruit, vegetables
Vitamin A	carrots, beetroot, tomatoes
Vitamin B Complex	wholegrains, seeds, nuts, vegetables, beans, lentils, eggs, skimmed milk, low-fat cheese, low-fat yoghurt
Vitamin C	berries, tropical fruits, peppers, all fresh fruit and vegetables
Vitamin D	fish, milk, egg yolk,
Vitamin E	wheatgerm, sunflower, safflower and walnut oils
Vitamin K	kelp, alfalfa, cauliflower, leafy green vegetables, polyunsaturated oils
Calcium	nuts, seeds, dairy foods
Chromium	brewer's yeast, mushrooms, wholewheat bread, beet sugar, molasses
Iron	oysters, green leafy vegetables, dried fruits, wholegrains, beans, lentils
Magnesium	green leafy vegetables, nuts, seeds,
Potassium	fruit - particularly bananas, vegetables
Selenium	nuts, seeds, wholegrains, fish
Sodium	fruit, vegetables
Zinc	nuts, seeds, wholegrains, wheatgerm

Fibre performs many important functions as well as controlling how quickly sugar enters the blood. It collects up toxins and helps to remove them from the body. Fibre also helps to prevent constipation; a problem many women experience in the week before a period, due to the presence of higher levels of hormones in the body.

Simple carbohydrates are found in refined and processed food. Confectionery and fizzy drinks are usually loaded with simple carbohydrates (sugars). Because these foods also contain little or no fibre the sugar from them is very rapidly released into the blood. This gives the body considerable work to do to keep the level of sugar in the blood within a normal limit. Excess sugar is associated with obesity, heart disease and diabetes.

Fats

Fats basically fall into two types: essential fats and non essential fats. It is important to remember that whatever the type of fat that is eaten, the body needs very little of it.

Essential Fats must be eaten in the diet, the body cannot make them. They are found mainly in polyunsaturated oils, nuts, seeds and wholegrains. Good quality cold-pressed oils, such as sunflower, sesame and walnut oils are rich sources of these essential oils. Essential fats go on to make important substances in the body called prostaglandins.

Certain types of prostaglandins are involved in keeping the blood thin and free from clots. Eating too much high-fat meat, high-fat dairy foods and sugar can block their action. Fish eat algae which is high in essential polyunsaturated oil. Eating fish gives us the benefit of these oils in a more concentrated and usable form, as the fish has already started the conversion process to make beneficial prostaglandins.

Non-essential fats can be made in the body from other substances. They are known as saturated fats and are not essential to eat. They are found mostly in meat, dairy food and eggs. Saturated fats are mainly used as an energy source for the body and are stored away as fat. A little in the diet should do no harm. Excess is linked to obesity, heart disease, breast cancer, allergies and arthritis.

Olive oil, although not an essential fat, contains many beneficial properties and those countries where it forms a natural part of the diet show a lower incidence of heart disease.

How to use fats

Essential fats - Use sparingly and where possible do not cook with them. Polyunsaturated oils are damaged very easily when they are heated and not only lose their beneficial properties, but can be harmful to the body. Damaged polyunsaturated oils are linked to the development of cancer, arthritis and heart disease. It is particularly important not to fry with these oils, although baking temperatures are less hazardous. Buy polyunsaturated oils and nuts and seeds in small quantities and store them in the fridge.

The same applies to margarines that are made from polyunsaturated oils. They are not suitable for cooking. The harder a margarine is, the more harmful it is. To make a margarine from an oil it has to become solid. The process of making a margarine solid is called hydrogenation. This chemical process alters the beneficial nature of the original polyunsaturated oil. Vitaquell and Vitasieg are two margarines that have been solidified through an emulsification process rather than hydrogenation. They can be be used as a spread, but are not suitable for cooking.

Eating a raw salad each day, tossed with a good quality polyunsaturated oil dressing and sprinkled with a few fresh seeds and a slice of wholegrain bread, should supply the body with sufficient essential oil to regulate hormones.

Non-essential fats are much more stable and are not easily damaged by heat. Butter and olive oil are therefore safer for cooking, though best kept to a minimum.

Best sources of protein

Whatever type of protein that you eat, the body will break it down in the digestive tract and use it to rebuild what it needs in the blood.

Nuts, seeds and vegetables supply good levels of protein in a way that helps to keep the body healthy. These foods contain alkaline minerals which help to balance high acid levels in protein. They provide more than enough protein to make healthy balanced hormones.

High protein sources include meat, dairy foods, fish, eggs, nuts, seeds, grains and pulses. However, meat, dairy foods, and eggs contain particularly high amounts of the acids that must be eliminated by the body. In order for the body to get rid of these undesirable acids it uses up valuable nutrients. The liver and the kidneys are also over worked in trying to break down the nitrogen and to eliminate the acids from the body. It is advisable to reduce the amount of high acid foods like meat, and replace them with grains and pulses which contain only moderate levels of these acids. Fruits and vegetables also contain acids, but they are in a form that is very easy for the body to dispose of.

Compared to vegetables, we need only small amounts of these sources of protein. Vegetarians and vegans fare very well without any meat and are usually very healthy.

Water forms about 90% of most fruit and vegetables. When 80% of the food that we eat comes from fruit and vegetables it provides water in a particularly beneficial form that best helps to cleanse the body, and carry enzymes, hormones and nutrients to the cells.

Drinking at least half a pint of plain water a day between each meal, in addition to eating a plentiful supply of fruit and vegetables, should supply an optimal level of water to keep the body healthy.

Tea, coffee and fizzy drinks are not the answer to increasing water in the body. Although these fluids are water-based they ultimately deplete the body of water and minerals.
• Good alternatives to tea include rooibosh tea, herb teas, luaka tea, fruit teas.
• Good alternatives to coffee include Caro, Barley cup.
• Good alternatives to fizzy drinks include Aqua Libra, Amé, Elderflower, Appletise, Rico, diluted fruit juice.

Quality versus quantity

It is clear that fruits, vegetables and water should form the basis of the *Diet For Life*. Most diets contain these essential ingredients, but not all foods supply them in a way that the body can use best. It is important to understand that the body will do its utmost to keep you well, irrespective of the quality of food that you eat. However, eating poor quality food gives your body a lot of extra work and that can ultimately lead to a break down in your health. Obtaining these essential ingredients from a wide variety of natural foods gives the body the least work to do and maximises your potential for health.

8
DEALING WITH STRESS CANDIDIASIS AND ALLERGIES

S ex hormones rarely become imbalanced for a single reason. It is usually a variety of factors that come together to create a problem. Common symptoms associated with PMS and the menopause can include insomnia, irritability, depression, poor concentration, joint pains and lack of sex drive. These symptoms are also inextricably linked with the symptoms of general nutrient deficiencies, stress, candidiasis and allergies.

Dealing with stress

Stress is a popular word that is used to describe a variety of problems. Women experience stress differently. Some women enjoy stress, others perform badly under it, and there are those that feel stressed because there isn't enough stress in their lives. It is difficult to measure how stressed a person is because of the variety of responses to it. However, whatever the stressor, the body will respond to it in the same way.

Modern day stressors include

- work pressures
- separation
- redundancy
- arguments
- food allergies

- coffee
- tea
- unemployment
- smoking
- noise

The body responds to a stressor by releasing a variety of chemicals to deal with the situation. The adrenal glands release adrenaline, which releases stored sugar into the blood. The sugar is then taken from the blood to the cells with the aid of the hormone insulin and GTF which contains the mineral chromium and vitamin B3, to be burnt for energy to deal with a perceived emergency. Stressors are not usually life-threatening, but come in the form of emotional problems and stimulants. Sugar that is not used up can be stored as fat in the body.

As part of this reaction, calcium is released from it's store in the bones in preparation for an immediate 'fight'. If the body doesn't clearly receive the message that the emergency is over then calcium does not get called back into the bones, which can contribute to osteoporosis.

Stimulants and continual stressors cause a sudden and rapid increase in blood sugar that is followed shortly afterwards by low blood sugar level. This is known as glucose intolerance.

Avoid stimulants and excess sugar and incorporate plenty of wholegrains, vegetables, some nuts and seeds and exercise into your daily routine. Vitamins B6, B5, B3, C and the minerals zinc, calcium and chromium are key nutrients that regulate this cycle.

Symptoms of glucose intolerance

- irritability
- anxiety
- insomnia
- depression
- dizziness
- mood swings
- poor concentration

Dealing with candidiasis

Candidiasis is excessive growth of a yeast organism called candida albicans, which is a normal inhabitant of the bowel. Unless encouraged to multiply, candida is not harmful. It flourishes on a diet of on sugars, yeasts and moulds. These foods include alcohol, confectionery, processed foods, dried fruits, bread, mushrooms, marmite, pickles and vinegars.

If this yeast organism flourishes it can develop a root to it's structure which can penetrate the bowel wall making it more 'leaky'. This can allow the candida into the blood stream along with other unwanted substances. Once in the blood, candida tends to settle where the person is weakest. A common site is in the joints, leading to joint pains.

Many of the symptoms of candidiasis arise as a result of an increased level of toxins in the blood and include:

Symptoms of candidiasis

- headaches
- irritability
- anxiety
- depression
- joint aches
- insomnia

- anal irritation
- bloating
- flatulence
- mood swings
- dizziness
- oral and vaginal thrush

If you suspect you may have candidiasis then the 'Beat Candida Cookbook' by Erica White provides a full explanation and treatment programme for this condition. See recommended reading on page 94. Working with a nutritionist is the best way of dealing with candidiasis.

Dealing with allergies

Food allergies are likely to occur when the lining of the bowel wall is more leaky than it should be. Foods can act as local irritants on the bowel wall and make it more porous. If larger particles of food escape into the blood stream through the bowel wall, the immune system sees them as 'foreign' and sets up an inflammatory reaction. Headaches and joint pains may result. It also gives the body a stress signal which can give rise to all the problems described under *Dealing With Stress* on page 61.

Sometimes it is not a true allergy that exists, but a food intolerance. The symptoms and treatment are similar. A true allergy will set up an immune reaction. A food intolerance often results from overuse of a food like wheat and does not usually directly involve the immune system. Common food offenders include bread, pasta, pastries, milk , cheese and citrus fruits.

If you suspect a food reaction, try avoiding all wheat and dairy foods for two weeks. After a few days of withdrawal symptoms you should start to feel better. After two weeks eat a large amount of wheat at one meal and observe how you feel over the next three days. Three days later, follow the same procedure to test for dairy foods. If you find your symptoms get worse, avoid the food for a further 3 months and then try again. If there is no reaction, bring small amounts slowly back into your diet.

It is very important that you replace these major foods with suitable alternatives that will replace the nutrients lost by their exclusion. Read labels on food to ensure that they are free from wheat and dairy foods.

Alternatives to wheat include corn pasta, rye pasta, rice pasta, rice cakes, rye crackers, oat cakes, brown rice, wholegrain cornflakes, porridge oats, millet flakes.

Alternatives to dairy foods are soya milk, tofu, soya cheese, nuts, seeds, green leafy vegetables.

9
SPECIAL NUTRITION PROGRAMMES

A lthough *The Diet For Life* will help improve general health, there are some special health conditions that require some extra help. These nutrition programmes are intended as a supplement to the *Diet For Life*. Each programme has specific information relating to that condition, and you may also be asked to follow the recommendations in the appropriate sections in the previous chapter for *Dealing With Stress*, *Dealing With Candidiasis* and *Dealing With Allergies*..

It is advisable to take supplements with food, unless specifically directed otherwise, and the indications in the programme are for breakfast (am) and dinner (pm). The supplement programmes are based on a high strength multivitamin/mineral supplement. available in health stores, and 1 gram of vitamin C. This is a good level of supplementation to support the *Diet For Life*. When supplementing calcium and magnesium use amino acid chelates or citrates.

A word of caution: if you are currently planning for a pregnancy, have any major disease, or are regularly taking medications, including synthetic hormones, then please consult a nutritionist or a nutritional doctor first.

Also, vitamin E should not be supplemented above 100iu if you have high blood pressure.

Painful periods

Painful periods are not uncommon, particularly in young women before they have had a baby. Many women gain relief from following a general optimum nutrition programme as outlined in the *Diet For Life* and dealing with allergies and or candidiasis.

The muscles of the womb, like other muscles in the body, can become imbalanced in their ability to contract and relax. At the time of a period the womb is shedding its inner lining, so the muscles are working extra hard to do this and to help control the bleeding. Calcium and magnesium are the two major nutrients needed to control this process. Eating healthy foods rich in calcium and magnesium, and taking supplements, has helped many women. Essential polyunsaturated oils, vitamin E and the mineral zinc may also help. It is worth taking some supplements to boost your intake of these nutrients. Essential polyunsaturated oils are particularly likely to help if the pain is associated with a heavy loss that has a tendency to clot. Essential polyunsaturated oils make a type of prostaglandin that controls blood thickness. Prostaglandins also balance muscle contraction in the womb, which can result in abdominal cramps. Taking extra vitamin E should help this. Vitamin E can assist by inhibiting the action of this type of prostaglandin by improving the blood circulation and bringing extra oxygen to the womb, so that when the womb contracts, more blood and oxygen will pass through. It is this potential lack of blood and oxygen that is thought to be partly responsible for menstrual cramps. Cutting down on eating red meat and dairy produce should also help, as these high fat foods can interfere with prostaglandin balance.

The contraceptive pill is often recommended for period pains. Nutritionally-oriented doctors do not recommend this approach as the Pill interferes with the working of many essential nutrients. Many women recover from painful periods naturally with help from those same nutrients that are depleted by the Pill.

Supplement programme to help painful periods

	AM	PM
Multivitamin/mineral	1	
Vitamin C with bioflavonoids 1000mg	1	
*Calcium 500mg Magnesium 250mg		1
Zinc (as citrate) 15mg		1
Vitamin E 200iu	1	
+Evening primrose oil 1 gram	1	

* Take 2 on the day before and after your period starts
+ Take 2 during the last 2 weeks of your cycle

Heavy periods

Follow the *Diet For Life* on page 61 and address potential food intolerances. Some women find that their periods get heavier in the first few months of an anti-candida diet, but it usually settles down.

One study showed that heavy periods may be caused by a deficiency of vitamin A. Vitamin A levels appear to fluctuate over the month, indicating a correlation with the fluctuating female hormones.

Another study clearly indicates that women with heavy periods had less than half the normal levels of vitamin A in the blood stream. Researchers found that when treating heavy periods with high levels of vitamin A daily for 35 days, over half of the participants' heavy periods were completely cured, and 14 more women showed a marked improvement. In all, 93% improved.

Sometimes it may not be that vitamin A is actually deficient. It is a fat-soluble vitamin that is stored in the liver. Since both zinc and vitamin E are needed to make use of stores of vitamin A, a lack of these can induce vitamin A deficiency.

The contraceptive pill often creates a high level of vitamin A in the blood and while taking the Pill a woman's periods are usually fine. The Pill creates this high level of vitamin A in the blood by moving it from it's store in the liver. When a woman stops taking the Pill the level of vitamin A in the blood can fall dramatically which leads to the stores of vitamin A in the liver also being depleted. It is common to experience heavy periods after stopping the Pill.

Vitamin A is a fat-soluble vitamin, supplied in fats and oils. Vitamin A as retinol is potentially toxic at high levels, and is best avoided if considering a pregnancy or pregnant. Vitamin A from animal sources (retinol) is twice as potent as vitamin A from vegetables sources (beta carotene).

Vitamin C and bioflavonoids have been shown to help control heavy periods. Bioflavonoids are found mainly just beneath the surface skin of fruit.

It is unclear whether low iron levels are an effect , as well as a cause, of heavy periods. Correcting low iron levels is an essential part of the programme. Taking vitamin C with iron rich foods increases the absorption of iron.

Supplement programme to help heavy periods

	AM	PM
Multivitamin/mineral	1	
Vitamin C with Bioflavonoids 1000mg	1	
Beta-carotene 25,000iu	1	
Zinc (as citrate) 15mg		1
Vitamin E 200iu	1	
Iron (as bisglycinate) 30 mg	1	

Irregular periods and fertility

Depending on the cause, irregular periods can be perfectly normal. Towards the menopause it is expected that periods will become irregular. When pregnant it is expected that periods will stop. If you are not pregnant or nearing the menopause and your periods are either absent or irregular it is worth checking out the cause.

Periods become irregular towards the menopause due to the declining levels of sex hormones. Absent or irregular periods are associated with low weight, strenuous exercise, anorexia nervosa, taking the contraceptive pill, or extreme stress. Extreme stress can lead to either missed periods or more frequent periods. Follow the *Diet For Life* and *Dealing With Stress* on pages 61 and 65.

Fertility Absence of periods is a major cause of infertility. A good supply of all nutrients is essential for fertility. A woman who is below 15% of her ideal body weight increases her risks for becoming infertile. To maintain regular periods and fertility, it appears that about 22% body fat is required.

Loss of periods is not uncommon in young women athletes who have a hard training schedule. If trying to conceive, it would be sensible to change to a less demanding regime. Similarly, the slimming disease anorexia nervosa often presents with absence of periods as part of the overall picture. Low levels of zinc have repeatedly been found in anorexia sufferers. Studies have shown that correcting the zinc deficiency has helped reverse the condition. Zinc is vital for our sense of taste and smell, which ultimately affects appetite. Zinc is vital for the production of sex hormones.

Eating a well-balanced diet is a key factor in maintaining an ideal weight. When the body is supplied with the nutrients needed to burn up the foods that we eat, it is much easier for it to stabilise weight. Infertility due to poor nutrition is not uncommon. Almost half of the women attending clinics complaining of a loss of periods are there because of the effects of dieting.

Vitamin A, vitamin C and the amino acid cysteine, found in dairy foods, onions, garlic and eggs are also vital for the production of sex hormones. B vitamins are essential for fertility, particularly vitamins B6 and B12. Studies have shown that supplementing B6 and B12 have significantly improved fertility.

A balanced diet that includes foods naturally rich in oestrogens and progesterone should help improve fertility. Oestrogens are needed to ripen an egg ready for fertilisation. Progesterone is needed to support the fertilised egg.

Oestrogen- rich foods are tofu, citrus fruits, wholewheat, licorice, alfalfa, fennel and celery. Wild yams are a very rich source of progesterone.

An optimum diet is the first place to start for dealing with irregular periods and improving the chance of becoming fertile. Tackling candidiasis, stress and potential food allergies is the next step. Stopping smoking and drinking alcohol are also essential for fertility and a healthy pregnancy.

After stopping the contraceptive pill it can sometimes take up to two years to conceive, and a small percentage of women remain permanently infertile. The Pill interferes with many nutrients that are needed for supporting a pregnancy, and also hinders the body's ability to make prostaglandins, which are needed to regulate hormones.

Candidiasis is a common problem in women, particularly those taking the contraceptive pill. Research has shown that candidiasis is a common problem with women having difficulty conceiving. If you have candidiasis, then follow the programme for *Dealing with Candidiasis.*

Avoid an anti-candida diet unless you commit to treating the problem prior to becoming pregnant. During an anti-candida programme toxins are released and the effects of these on a developing infant are unknown.

Hostile, acidic cervical mucus is another cause of infertility. This is associated with toxicity which can create an acid and inhospitable environment for the sperm. Nutritional intervention can help this situation and following the *Diet*

For Life should help regulate the acidity of the cervical mucus by helping the body accumulate less toxins.

Supplement programme for regular periods & fertility

	AM	PM
Multivitamin/mineral	1	
Vitamin C with bioflavonoids 1000mg	1	
B Complex 50mg	1	
Zinc (as citrate) 15mg	1	
Beta-carotene 25,000iu	1	
Vitamin E 200iu	1	
Evening primrose oil 1 gram	1	

Fibrocystic breast disease

Cysts, or lumps, in the breast are experienced by between 20-50% of women. The breasts are tender and the cysts are moveable and usually near the surface of the breast. The problem usually progresses until the menopause and then subsides. It is mainly associated with too much oestrogen, particularly oestrone and oestradiol which are extremely active stimulants of breast tissue.

Food and drinks containing the chemical methylxanthine, as found in tea, coffee, cola and chocolate, aggravate the problem. Removing these items from your diet is advisable. A low-salt diet helps reduce breast tenderness and swelling.

Although most cysts are benign, women who do have cysts also have a greatly increased chance of developing breast cancer. Vitamins A, C, E and the minerals zinc and selenium are particularly protective against cancer. Follow the *Diet For Life* and recommendations for *Dealing With Stress*.

Supplement programme for fibrocystic breasts

	AM	PM
Multivitamin/mineral	1	
Vitamin C with bioflavonoids1000mg	1	
Beta carotene 25,000iu	1	
Vitamin E 100iu	1	
Zinc (as citrate) 15mg		1
Selenium 50mcg		1

Fibroids

Fibroids are the most common growths of the female reproductive system. They are benign, firm, round lumps that attach themselves to the muscular wall of the womb. There are usually more than one. They often grow to the size of a grapefruit and routinely disappear after the menopause.

Fibroids give rise to irregular, heavy and painful periods. The weight of the fibroids can weaken the pelvic floor muscles, leading to stress incontinence. The usual treatment is to surgically remove them.

Fibroids are strongly linked to too much oestrogen. Yam is a rich source of natural progesterone which should help redress the balance if taken as a food, or applied as a cream.

Follow the supplement programme and general diet advice recommended for fibrocystic breasts.

Ovarian cysts

Ovarian cysts result from a failure of normal egg development and disordered ovulation. Women in their mid-thirties onwards are more likely to develop ovarian cysts. Cysts can grow to the size of a golf ball and create considerable pain. These cysts result from failed ovulation and continue to grow under the influence of follicle stimulating hormone (FSH). Each month the rise of FSH is followed by a surge of luteinising hormone (LH) which causes the site of the follicle to swell and this stretches the surface of the ovary, causing pain and possible bleeding at the site. Treatment may result in surgery.

Dr Ellen Grant finds that the majority of her patients with ovarian cysts are deficient in zinc. She says that when zinc is in short supply certain types of cysts can develop, possibly because zinc is required for the growth of the egg. In her experience, women are much more likely to develop ovarian cysts as a result of infertility drugs. Some of these drugs block oestrogen receptors and increase the output of FSH and LH when women are failing to ovulate.

Follow the *Diet for Life* on page 61 and supplement a high potency multivitamin/mineral plus an extra 15mg of zinc.

Endometriosis

Endometriosis is a very common and painful disease, the cause of which remains unknown. One in seven women is thought to suffer from endometriosis. Small fragments of endometrial tissue migrate into the muscular wall of the womb and out through the fallopian tubes. The fragments can be found on the surface of the ovaries and the contents of the pelvis, including the bowel. Endometrial tissue has been found in many distant sites of the body, well away from the womb and they respond to the natural fluctuations of oestrogens and progesterone. The fragments swell up with blood during the month and also bleed at the time of menstruation. Bleeding from these sites can occur at other times during the cycle. This can cause considerable pain, which often starts shortly before menstruation and does not subside until it is finished.Some women find that their pain increases at the time of ovulation.Endometriosis is a common cause of infertility and heavy and irregular bleeding. About 50% of women investigated for infertility have endometriosis. One study showed that women who had taken the Pill had nearly twice the incidence of endometriosis compared to women who had never taken it.

The following supplement programme is intended to be followed for at least 2-3 months and is recommended only for women who are not taking any hormone treatment. If you are taking hormones please consult a nutrionist before undertaking the programme.

Supplement programme for endemetriosis

	AM	PM
Multivitamin/mineral	1	
Vitamin C with bioflavonoids1000mg	1	
B Complex 50mg	1	
Vitamin E 200iu	1	
Zinc (as citrate) 20mg		1
Selenium 150mcg		1
Magnesium 400mg		1
Calcium 200mg		1

Pregnancy

Nutrition plays a very important part in pregnancy. If you wish to become pregnant, then it is wise to plan for the pregnancy. A 3-6 month investment in an optimum nutrition programme is well worth the effort, for you and for the health of your baby. Ideally your partner should join you and both partners are especially recommended to avoid smoking and alcohol.

Diet and pregnancy Food intake in pregnancy increases by 15-20%. The requirements for folic acid, vitamin B, C, calcium, zinc and magnesium increase by 30 -100 per cent. It is important that a mother chooses foods that are rich in nutrients, and not simply high in calories.

Even the best of diets does not provide the correct levels of all the nutrients needed for pregnancy. Studies show that mothers who supplement their diet with nutrients reduce by 75% their risk of having a baby with congenital abnormalities. Folic acid has now been confirmed as essential in preventing spina bifida. It is wise to take a specially prepared pregnancy formula, as they have been designed to meet both the mother's needs during pregnancy, and that of her developing baby. Key nutrients to supplement during pregnancy are vitamin B12, B6, folic acid, zinc and iron.

Miscarriage and pregnancy Often women are sufficiently fertile to become pregnant, but are unable to maintain the pregnancy. Deficiencies of essential polyunsaturated oils, zinc, manganese and vitamin E are associated with recurrent miscarriages. Other causes of miscarriage include diabetes, thyroid problems and infections such as cytomegalovirus, chlamydia and herpes. High levels of toxic metals like lead and cadmium are also implicated. Low levels of progesterone are linked to miscarriage as progesterone is needed to support the fertilised egg. Eating yam, a rich source of natural progesterone-like substances, is recommended in this situation, as is using natural progesterone cream.

Morning sickness In my experience women that experience morning sickness during pregnancy are relieved by changing to *The Diet For Life* given on page 61. Dealing with stress and food cravings, and following a diet to balance glucose levels in the blood, does help many women. Also follow the dietary recommendations given for *Dealing With Stress* on page 65. Morning sickness usually stops around 12-14 weeks of pregnancy. If it persists beyond 14 weeks of pregnancy you should seek medical advice. Morning sickness has been shown to respond to 50mg of vitamin B6 twice a day and 200-500mg of magnesium once a day.

Cravings Low zinc levels are associated with the abnormal cravings a pregnant woman often experiences in early pregnancy. In addition, replenishing low iron levels in the body has been successfully used to control abnormal cravings that some women experience for strange, and sometimes harmful, substances such as chalk or coal.

Thrush Is more common during pregnancy. Eating an optimum diet should reduce this tendency. If you have thrush, limit sugars, yeasts and moulds in the diet, as outlined in *Dealing With Candidiasis* on page 66. A full anti-candida programme should be avoided when pregnant. If you suspect that candidiasis is your problem then consult your health practitioner for guidance.

Constipation and varicose veins Often occur together and are more common in pregnancy due to changes in hormone levels, which make the muscles more relaxed. A good wholefood diet containing plenty of fibre is beneficial. Some women who develop varicose veins have been shown to be low in vitamin B6.

Urinary infections This a common condition. The ureters become more relaxed and urine can stagnate. Drinking plenty of plain water helps reduce this tendency.

Pre-eclampsia Studies show that women who received a daily supplement of vitamin B6 10mg, had a significantly lower incidence of pre-eclampsia (toxaemia of pregnancy), than those who did not. Pre-eclampsia is recognised by the appearance of protein in the urine, increasing blood pressure, water retention and weight gain. Low levels of zinc have also been found in women with pre-eclampsia.

Blood Pressure Raised blood pressure commonly occurs in pregnancy and an optimum diet should help to control it. Evening primrose oil and calcium have both been used successfully to reduce blood pressure in pregnancy.

Heartburn Antacids commonly given for heartburn often contain aluminium. Some evidence has shown that this can be toxic. A quarter of a teaspoonful of sodium bicarbonate dissolved in water and taken between meals can bring relief, but a change of diet is a priority.

Supplement programme in pregnancy

	AM	PM
Multivitamin	1	
Multimineral (containing iron 10mg)	1	
Vitamin C 1000mg	1	
Beta carotene 8000ius		1
B12 25mcg	1	
Folic acid 200mcg (minimum)	1	
Biotin 100mcg	1	
B6 100mg	1	
Zinc (as citrate) 15mg		1
Evening primrose oil 1 gram		1

Caution: Vitamin A as retinol above 7500ius should be avoided during pregnancy.

Premenstrual syndrome (PMS)

PMS is a collection of symptoms which may begin during the two weeks prior to a period and usually pass within an hour to a few days after menstruation starts. Common symptoms include anxiety, irritability, fluid retention, mood swings, bloating, breast tenderness, weight gain, acne, fatigue, sweet cravings and forgetfulness.

It is not necessary to experience all of these symptoms, but a sufficient collection of them is highly indicative that PMS is present. Following the basic *Diet For Life* on page 61 is essential. If symptoms persist, then follow the recommendations in the previous chapter for *Dealing With Stress*, *Dealing With Allergies* and *Dealing With Candidiasis* in that order. Very often most symptoms of PMS have disappeared after implementing these strategies.

There are several types of PMS that have a different collection of symptoms, and these often overlap.

PMS associated with high oestrogen and low progesterone levels. This is the category that 75% of PMS sufferers fall into. B6 in the range of 200-800mg reduced blood oestrogen, increased progesterone and reduced symptoms in a clinical trial. Eating wild yams, which contain naturally high levels of progesterone-like substances, should also be of benefit.

PMS associated with food cravings This type of PMS affects about 30% of sufferers. Women with this type of PMS can tolerate an increased amount of carbohydrate foods. They usually have a low level of magnesium in their red blood cells. Often essential polyunsaturated oils are deficient. Supplementing magnesium improves cravings and shows improvements in other symptoms too. Too much refined sugar causes a loss of magnesium and chromium in the urine. Supplementing chromium helps control blood glucose levels. This type of PMS affects about 30% of sufferers.

PMS associated with water retention This type of PMS affects between 65-75% of sufferers. B6, magnesium and vitamin E have been shown to be helpful. Reducing sodium (salt) intake is also beneficial. Excess sodium increases the likelihood of developing water retention.

PMS associated with high progesterone levels In 25-35% of sufferers progesterone levels are higher than normal in the second half of the cycle. Such sufferers are prone to depression. Vitamin B6, C and magnesium may help.

Supplement programme for PMS

	AM	PM
Multivitamin/mineral	1	
Vitamin C 1000mg	1	
B Complex 50mg	1	
Calcium 500mg Magnesium 500mg	1	
Zinc (as citrate) 15mg		1
Vitamin E 100iu	1	
Chromium GTF 100mcg		1
Evening primrose oil 1 gram	1	1

Weight gain

When the body is supplied with an optimum quota of nutrients it responds by maintaining an even weight. The nutrients that are particularly needed for weight management include B vitamins, vitamin C, magnesium, zinc, selenium, iodine, iron, manganese, and chromium.

Follow the basic *Diet For Life* and *Dealing With Stress*. The next step to follow is *Dealing With Allergies* on page 67. It is often difficult for the body to maintain an ideal body weight if food allergic. A common symptom of food allergy is water retention. Many people experience a loss of 7lbs within a week by just removing an offending food. This is water loss, not fat loss, but makes big difference to how you feel.

A low functioning thyroid gland commonly results in excess weight. The minerals iodine and selenium have been shown to help the thyroid gland work more efficiently.

Exercise is vital. A brisk walk for 15 minutes, 3 times a

week can substantially increase how quickly foods are burnt up. Exercise is beneficial at all levels of health.

Some essential fats from a few nuts, seeds and wholegrains, can help burn fat rather than create it.

Supplement programme to stabilise weight

	AM	PM
Multivitamin	1	
Multimineral	1	
Vitamin C with bioflavonoids 1000mg	1	
B Complex 50mg	1	
Vitamin B3 100mcg	1	
Vitamin B6 100mg	1	
Zinc (as citrate) 15mg		1
Chromium GTF 100mcg		1

Pelvic inflammatory disease (PID)

PID is a serious inflammation of the uterus and fallopian tubes which can give rise to pelvic abscesses. It is usually treated with antibiotics. Surgery is not uncommon. Infection first occurs in the vagina and cervix and can ascend into the endometrium in the womb and along the fallopian tubes.

Prevention is better than cure. Increasing the body's resistance to opportunistic infections like candida and chlamydia is a high priority. This involves boosting your immune system and dealing with stress. Vital nutrients are vitamins C, E, A, B6, calcium, magnesium, zinc, selenium and essential oils. Follow the *Diet For Life* then follow the recommendations for *Dealing With Stress* and *Candidiasis*.

The correct balance of hormones should create normal vaginal mucus. As a woman nears the menopause oestrogen levels decline, increasing susceptibility to vaginal infections.

Women on the Pill are more susceptible to vaginal infections. It is unlikely that the contraceptive pill will favour normal mucus production as they do not contain oestriol which is beneficial to vaginal tissue. Beta-carotene, vitamins C and E are needed for normal mucus production.

Supplement programme for PID

	AM	PM
Multivitamin/mineral	1	
Vitamin C with bioflavonoids	1	1
Beta-carotene 25,000iu	1	
Vitamin E 200iu	1	
Vitamin B6 100mg	1	
Calcium 500mg Magnesium 250mg		1
Zinc (as citrate) 15mg		1
Evening primrose oil 1 gram	1	

Osteoporosis

Bone is an active living tissue which continually restores itself. A declining level of oestrogen allows the excessive release of parathyroid hormone which encourages calcium out of the bones and into the blood. This loss of calcium from the bones is compounded by the repeated intake of stimulants, a high protein diet and a stressful lifestyle.

Replacing oestrogens in the form of HRT is not really the answer. The cells that build new bone do not contain receptors for oestrogens. They do contain receptors for progesterone, the hormone needed for strong healthy bones.

Calcium is very important for bones, but the interaction of calcium with other essential nutrients is vital. Magnesium, phosphorous, vitamin K, boron, B6, sodium, and protein all have a major influence on the final depositing of calcium into bones. Dairy foods are rich in calcium but poor in magnesium, and so create a mineral imbalance. Eating nuts, seeds and vegetables gives a good supply of both, with the added advantage of creating a more alkaline environment in the blood. Excess protein leaches calcium from bone in order to neutralise acidity.

Follow the *Diet For Life* on page 61, followed by the recommendations for *Dealing With Stress*.

Weight-bearing exercise is vital for healthy bones. A fifteen minute brisk walk, three times a week is a good start.

Supplement programme to help improve bone health

	AM	PM
Multivitamin/mineral	1	
Vitamin C with bioflavonoids 1000mg		1
Full B Complex 50mg	1	
Calcium 500mg Magnesium 250mg	1	
Boron 3mg		1
Zinc (as citrate) 15mg	1	

Hot flushes

Three quarters of all British menopausal women experience some hot flushes, particularly those who are thin. Hot flushes are not directly a sign of oestrogen deficiency, but are a result of increased activity of the hypothalamus gland in the brain to bring about the production of the hormones, FSH and LH. High levels of these two hormones occur as the menopause approaches. They are working extra hard to stimulate any remaining eggs to grow and develop. Oestrogen and progesterone levels fall towards the menopause. Raising progesterone levels would increase receptors in oestrogen sensitive cells and reduce hot flushes.

Hot flushes may also be reduced by supplementing vitamin E combined with vitamin C and bioflavonoids. When vitamin E levels are low, there is a tendency for the hormones FSH and LH to increase. Vitamin E appears to stabilise the output of oestrogens.

Supplement programme to help control hot flushes

	AM	PM
Multivitamin/mineral	1	
Vitamin C with Bioflavonoids 1000mg	1	
Vitamin E up to 1000iu	1	
Evening primrose oil 1gram		1

Improving sex drive

A lack of sex drive can result from a variety of reasons, not all nutritional. However, improving nutrition may make you feel better, in turn having a favourable impact on how you feel about sex. The first place to start is by following the *Diet For Life*. The recommendations for *Dealing With Stress*, *Allergies* and *Candidiasis* can all make a difference.

Maintaining a healthy sex life The vagina is kept moist by encouraging the production of vaginal secretions. Keeping the adrenal glands healthy helps too, as declining oestrogen levels tend to dry up vaginal secretions. The adrenal glands continue to produce oestrogens, as do fat cells, during and after the menopause. Vitamin E cream used locally has helped many women with vaginitis. Supplementing vitamins A and C, plus zinc are also important for keeping vaginal membranes healthy.

Vaginitis and the Pill Vaginitis is more common with women that take the Pill. It is possible that it prevents the normal protective vaginal mucus from being produced.

Vaginitis and natural hormone creams Oestrogen creams have been successful in treating vaginitis and can also reduce the occurrence of urinary tract infections, restore normal vaginal mucus membranes, and provide the right environment in the vagina which inhibits the growth of unfriendly organisms. Dr Lee found that when these women used progesterone creams rubbed into the skin to treat their vaginitis, they showed a similar benefit to those using oestrogen cream.

Supplement programme for a healthy sex life

	AM	PM
Multivitamin/mineral	1	
Vitamin C with bioflavonoids1000mg	1	
B Complex 50mg	1	
Vitamin E 200iu	1	
Beta-carotene 25,000iu	1	
Zinc (as citrate) 15mg		1

Depression

The causes of depression are many and some types can be helped with nutrition. Causes of hormone imbalance can be B vitamin deficiency, stress, imbalance between calcium and magnesium, allergies, candidiasis, imbalance between oestrogens and progesterone. For more information about hormone imbalance and depression please refer to page 40.

10
NATURAL HORMONES - HOW TO USE THEM

Natural hormone programmes are given for pre-menstrual syndrome, the menopause and osteoporosis. If you suffer from endometriosis, ovarian cysts, fibrocystic breasts, fibroids, absence of periods or wish to become pregnant, it is best to see a nutritionist who can give you personal advice.

Cautions

Some women report incidental 'spotting' with progesterone use. This is usually temporary. Any persistent spotting or breakthrough bleeding should be reported to your doctor. Likewise if you experience headaches or other progressive symptoms be sure to consult your doctor.

If you take thyroid medication then please consult your practitioner as progesterone increases thyroid activity and you may require a lower dose of thyroid hormone.

Oestrogen supplementation is not advisable for women with diabetes, varicose veins, a high blood fat level, high blood pressure, fibrocystic breasts, obesity, a history of breast cancer, endometrial cancer and any clotting disorders.

Postmenopausal women taking an oestrogen as HRT should reduce the dosage of HRT by a third to a half when starting natural progesterone. Otherwise they are likely to experience the symptoms of oestrogen dominance during the first two months of progesterone use.

Using natural hormones

Massage progesterone and oestrogen creams into the skin until they are well absorbed. The creams can be applied to any area of the body, but are best absorbed where the skin is thinner such as the neck, chest, breasts, lower abdomen, inner thighs, wrists and inner arms. Regularly rotate the application of the creams to different parts of the body for maximum effect.

Natural progesterone is available as a cream in a 2oz jar or as an oil in a 1 ounce bottle. The oil and the cream can be used together for treating persistent menopausal problems like hot flushes.

Natural progesterone oil can be taken directly under the tongue or, if you don't like the taste, it can be rubbed into the soles of the feet. If you use this method, apply the oil at night

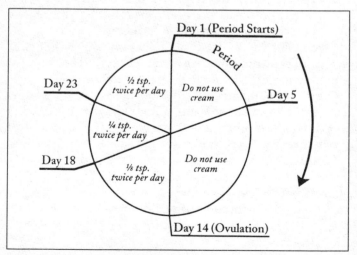

Figure 5: Premenstrual syndrome

and wear old socks to prevent any staining from the oil going onto the bed clothes.

Natural oestrogen is available as a cream and comes in a 2oz jar. Natural oestrogen is also available in tablet form.

Pre-menstrual syndrome Natural progesterone cream helps reduce common symptoms associated with PMS. The cream is used in a way that would simulate the natural menstrual cycle. (see figure 5)

Menopause The amount of cream recommended here is only a guide. All women respond to the menopause differently, some with mild and some with acute symptoms. Each woman's requirements for progesterone will vary, so start with the guidelines and adjust the level to meet your needs. If you have stopped menstruating, use the same schedule but base it on the calendar month (see figure 6).

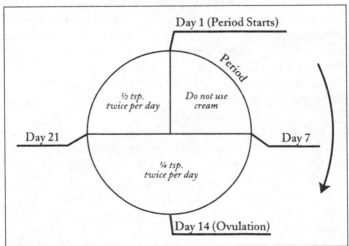

Figure 6: Menopause

Natural progesterone and persistent vaginal dryness and hot flushes Natural progesterone cream used vaginally has been very successful in treating vaginal dryness in women. For vaginal dryness and discomfort insert a quarter to half a teaspoon once a day. This may be added to your usual daily application.

For hot flushes use extra natural progesterone cream for immediate relief of symptoms. Use a quarter to half a teaspoon every fifteen minutes for one hour following the hot flush.

When menopausal symptoms remain persistent the progesterone oil is more effective. For hot flushes, place 2-5 drops of the oil under the tongue and retain it for five minutes. Repeat the dose every ten to fifteen minutes for the hour following the hot flush. The oil may also be rubbed into the soles of the feet.

Natural oestrogen and menopausal problems Some doctors estimate that between 10-15% of their patients need supplementing with natural oestrogen, as well as natural progesterone, to help alleviate persistent menopausal symptoms. If you are recommended to use natural oestrogen cream it is best to simulate the normal menstrual cycle and use it in conjunction with natural progesterone. Use oestrogen cream on days 3-25 and progesterone cream on days 10-25, and use nothing for five to seven days. For maximum effectiveness, apply oestrogen and progesterone at different times; progesterone in the morning and oestrogen in the evening. Start with a quarter of a teaspoon of oestrogen cream per day and slowly increase it until symptoms are controlled. Once controlled reduce the amount of oestrogen cream and maintain at the minimum required to remain symptom free.

Oestrogen cream may be used vaginally to relieve vaginal

dryness, pain, itching and atrophy. Insert a quarter of a teaspoon of cream into the vagina, and around the area immediately outside it, for seven consecutive days. If symptoms continue the cream may be inserted once a week to alleviate the problem.

Osteoporosis

It is a good idea to find out how severe your bone loss is before starting natural progesterone cream and then check yearly whether the situation has improved. Having a test for osteoporosis is not vital in order to use the cream.

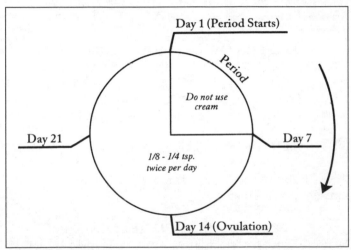

Figure 7: Osteoporosis

If you have severe osteoporosis or have experienced fractures, then double the dose of progesterone cream over the same time span given. (See figure 7.)

USEFUL ADDRESSES

NATURAL FAMILY PLANNING CENTRE, *Birmingham Maternity Hospital, Q.E. Medical Centre, Birmingham B15 2TG* Gives advice about how to control fertility naturally.

THE INSTITUTE FOR OPTIMUM NUTRITION, *5 Jerdan Place, Fulham SW6 1BE.* Offers personal consultations with qualified nutritionists, including Kate Neil. On request ION will send you a free information pack. A directory of nutrition consultants is also available (price £1.50)

KATE NEIL is available for consultation at: *ION Tel: 071 385 7984: Heath Health Care, Hampstead, London. Tel: 071 267 4222: Bracknell Centre, Bracknell, Berkshire Tel: 0344 483755.*

SUPPLIERS OF NATURAL HORMONES

HIGHER NATURE, *The Nutrition Centre, Burwash Common, East Sussex TN19 7LX Tel: 0435 882880.* Distribute Pro-Gest cream and oil from Mexican Yam, and Es-Gen cream, an extract of soy. These products are available through practitioners.

NUTRI-CENTRE, *Hale Clinic, 7 Park Crescent, London W1N 3HE Tel: 071 436 5122* Distribute Phytoestrol tablets, derived from rhubarb and hops. These products are available through practitioners.

RECOMMENDED READING

Natural Family Planning Dr Anna M Flynne & Melissa Brooks (Unwin Paperbacks)

Natural Progesterone Dr John Lee available from ION

Optimum Nutrition Patrick Holford (ION Press)

Sexual Chemistry Dr Ellen Grant (Cedar)

The Beat Candida Cookbook Erica White available from ION

This amended INDEX replaces the published index which contains incorrect page references.

I. O. N.

The Institute for Optimum Nutrition is a non profit-making independent organisation that exists to help you promote your health through nutrition. ION was founded in 1984 and is based in London. ION offers educational courses starting with a one-day introductory course right up to a three year training to become a nutrition consultant; a clinic for one-to-one consultations; publications and ION's magazine, Optimum Nutrition, which goes out free to members. If you'd like to receive more details please complete the details below.

Please send me your:

☐ FREE Information Pack
☐ Homestudy Course prospectus
☐ ION Clinic details
☐ Directory of Nutrition Consultants (enclose £1.50)

I'd like to order the following books: *(please list title, quantity & price)*

_____

_____

_____

I enclose £ _____ payable to ION (Please add 10% for p&p)

First Name: _____ Surname: _____

Address: _____

_____

_____ Post Code: _____

Now send this to: ION, 5 Jerdan Place, London SW6 1BE
(Tel: 071 385 7984)